Pretty PAINTED FURNITURE

D IANE T RIERWEILER

NORTH LIGHT BOOKS

CINCINNATI, OHIO

www.artistsnetwork.com

Library of Congress Cataloging-in-Publication Data

Trierweiler, Diane,
 Pretty painted furniture / Diane Trierweiler.
  p. cm.
 ISBN 1-58180-234-X (alk. paper)
 1. Furniture painting. I. Title.

TT199.4.T75 2002
749--dc21   2002016510

Editor: Maureen Mahany Berger
Production Coordinator: Kristen Heller
Designer: Joanna Detz
Layout artist: Linda Watts
Photographers: Christine Polomsky & Al Parrish

METRIC CONVERSION CHART

TO CONVERT	TO	MULTIPLY BY
Inches	Centimeters	2.54
Centimeters	Inches	0.4
Feet	Centimeters	30.5
Centimeters	Feet	0.03
Yards	Meters	0.9
Meters	Yards	1.1
Sq. Inches	Sq. Centimeters	6.45
Sq. Centimeters	Sq. Inches	0.16
Sq. Feet	Sq. Meters	0.09
Sq. Meters	Sq. Feet	10.8
Sq. Yards	Sq. Meters	0.8
Sq. Meters	Sq. Yards	1.2
Pounds	Kilograms	0.45
Kilograms	Pounds	2.2
Ounces	Grams	28.4
Grams	Ounces	0.04

About the author

Diane Trierweiler began teaching herself to paint in watercolor and oils in 1980. Encouraged by her husband, Gil, Diane took a decorative painting class, and after that class she said that she would one day open a decorative painting store. In 1986 her dream came true, and The Tole Bridge opened its doors in Norco, California. Today, Diane teaches decorative painting and fine art throughout the U.S. and Canada. Diane works in many different styles, using oils, acrylics and watercolor. She has been a member of the Society of Decorative Painters since 1985. She has had four books published, *Diane Paints Victorian Treasures, Country Lane Flower Shop, Painting Country Cottages and Gardens,* and *The Secret Garden*, has produced almost one hundred pattern packets and four videos for the Perfect Palette Studio. Diane has her own line of specialty brushes designed to make it easier for the student to paint landscapes and flowers. She has a wonderful husband, Gil, and two beautiful grown children named Jami and Jared. She lives in Southern California.

Dedication

I would like to dedicate this book to all of the great friends and students that I have met at my shop, The Tole Bridge, in Norco, California. And especially to my two dearest friends, Dian Deakins and Debbie De La Cruz. Dear friends like these are hard to find. Their support and encouragement were always there. I would also like to say how much I appreciate the support of my husband and my son in pursuing my love of painting.

Acknowledgments

Many, many thanks to Christine Polomsky, who did the great photography for this book; to Kathy Kipp, who had the confidence in me to publish my second book with North Light; and to Maureen Mahany Berger, my editor, who was there from the very beginning—patiently taking notes while I painted. Thanks, Maureen, for your input, suggestions and good taste. Your help was most appreciated.

Table of Contents

Introduction

When you first start painting on furniture pieces or on walls, you need to gather up resources. These could be swatches of wallpaper, carpet or fabrics, pictures from magazines or stationery, and many other things that you have around you all day long. Everyone needs inspiration! Stroll through designer stores and especially stores that feature painted furniture. Make notes of what appeals to you.

The next step is simply getting started. Say that your grandmother left you her old vanity table but the finish on it is not so good. You'd like to give it a "facelift" and put it in your daughter's room as a memento. One place to start is to consider what's popular in decorating. Right now Shabby Chic, Garden, and Country French are very popular. So you might consider giving the vanity one or two coats of light paint and simply sanding off the edges. Don't worry about the nicks and bumps in the surface—let them add character to the piece. Most pieces of furniture look nice with a little trim work of color on them. Painting the routered edge around a piece or taping off a strip around each drawer to be painted with a trim color adds interest. For grandmother's vanity, a small design on each drawer and perhaps on one corner of the top surface would be sufficient.

Sometimes the shape of the piece will inspire a more elaborate design. For instance, the dressing screen in this book (project 10) has a curved top edge, so it gave me the feeling of an arbor. It could have been a rose or a grape arbor instead of wisteria flowers.

If you have a large piece with drawers, like a dresser, you don't need to paint each drawer with a separate design. Consider treating the whole front surface as if it were one large flat area, like I have done on the chest at left. Why not paint a landscape or a seascape or a basket of flowers over the surface? Go ahead and take a chance! You can always paint over it if you don't like it. You will discover skills you didn't think you had.

In this book, I have supplied patterns for the designs I've painted. But I encourage my students to use the basic pattern to create their own designs. So, if you copy the basic structure of pattern, try painting the pattern in different colors or on different backgrounds to give it an entirely different feel. This idea can be applied not only to furniture but to anything you paint.

Getting Started

PAINTS

Acrylic paints are simply pigments suspended in water and resin. When applied to an object, the water evaporates, leaving the pigment and resin in place.

Curing time for acrylics is about seven days (this is also true for water-based varnishes). Unlike watercolor and gouache, once the acrylic is dry and cured, it will not move.

Most often, I use DecoArt Americana acrylics. The intensity of many of the DecoArt acrylic colors creates the look of an oil painting. Even when water is added to these acrylics, the pigments remain strong.

PALETTE

I like to lay my paints out on sheets of deli wrap with a moistened shop towel or a shop sponge underneath. The bright blue color of the shop towels under the deli wrap helps me to see my colors better.

To set up your palette, soak a shop towel or shop sponge in clean water. Lay this onto your palette. Lay a piece of deli wrap over the wet towel. The water will go through the deli wrap and keep your paints moist for a long time. Keep the towel or sponge wet by adding water to it now and then.

You can also blend your colors on the deli wrap without fear of picking up dried specks of paint.

Even though the paints will stay wet a lot longer on the wet palette, I only squeeze out a small portion of paint at a time.

PAINTING SUPPLIES

Shop towels are also good for absorbing the excess water from your brushes. They have very little lint, which prevents lint from transferring onto your work. The Loew-Cornell water tub has a partition in the middle to separate your clean and dirty water. You need a palette knife to mix your paints, although often paints are brush mixed.

Hint

If you're serious about painting, having a work space that is dedicated to your artwork is necessary. If you have to get all of your supplies out and set them up each time you want to paint, you may not paint as often.

To set up a good work space for painting, you will need good lighting, a comfortable chair and plenty of room to lay out your supplies.

BRUSHES

There are many brands and styles of brushes. Whatever brand you prefer, look for a quality golden Taklon brush. Taklon holds up better when using acrylic paints. You may prefer a mixed-bristle brush. These are made of half natural hair and half Taklon so they hold more water.

I like to use a natural-hair brush when painting trees and flowers in a landscape. The texture produced is softer and more muted than with a synthetic brush.

For this reason, I have designed Diane's Angel Series and Petal Series brushes. These are natural-hair short fan and mist brushes in a variety of sizes for painting foliage and flowers. They are available exclusively from The Tole Bridge, 1875 Norco Drive, Norco, CA 92860, (909) 272-6918.

BRUSH CARE

I always keep two Loew-Cornell brush tubs full of clean water next to me; constantly rinsing your brushes in dirty water will ruin them quickly.

Once I have thoroughly rinsed my brush, I always squeeze the water out of the bristles and reshape the chisel edge. Then I lay it down flat on a paper towel as I continue to paint. This keeps any dirty water from flowing up into the ferrule.

At the end of the painting session, I use DecoMagic brush cleaner to clean my acrylic brushes. Be sure to rinse the cleaner out of the brush before you paint again.

A good brush case is also necessary. Use one that opens up so that you can reach for your brushes without bending all of the other brush bristles. With proper care, your brushes should last a long time.

Some of My Brushes

Shown from top to bottom are Eagle series 1550 flat nos. 6 & 10, Eagle Millennium series 715 flat no. 10, Eagle Millennium series 710 ⅜-inch (10mm) and ½-inch (12mm) angles, Eagle Allure series 310 ⅝-inch (15mm) angle, Eagle Gold series 700 1½-inch (38mm) flat, Eagle Millennium series 770 ¾-inch (19mm) and 1½-inch (38mm) flats, Delta stencil brush, Diane's 10/0 striper, Diane's ½-inch (12mm) Angel Hair, Diane's ½-inch (12mm) Angel Mist, Diane's no. 4 Angel Wing, and Diane's Petal brushes nos. 2,4, 8 and ½-inch (12mm).

Furniture-painting Techniques

SIDE LOADING YOUR BRUSH

1 Dip your brush into water and blot on a paper towel. Pick up a tiny bit of paint on the corner of your brush.

2 Blend your brush in both directions on your palette.

3 Move slightly into the color using very little pressure. Keep your hand in the middle of the brush handle when you begin to float a color. Shadows become softer if you stay back on your brush handle.

LINEWORK

1 Add water to your paint and load the liner brush almost to the ferrule. Spin the brush to a point.

2 Stay up on the tip of the brush when painting.

DOUBLE LOADING

1 Turn your brush on its side and load into one color.

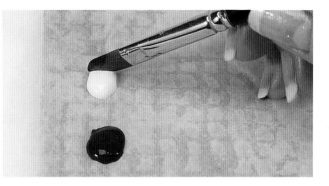

2 Turn your brush on its other side and load into a second color.

3 Blend on your palette.

4 Reverse direction and blend again. Keep the dark side of the brush on the dark side of the stroke.

ONE-STROKE LEAVES AND PETALS

1 To make a one-stroke figure, press down the whole flat edge of your double-loaded brush. Begin turning your brush and lifting as you move. These strokes may be painted singly or with two side-by-side strokes for leaves and flowers.

2 Raise the brush completely onto its chisel edge and pull away.

DOUBLE LOADING AN ANGEL WING BRUSH

1 Dip half of your brush into one color of paint. Dip the other half of your brush into a second color.

2 Pounce your brush out on the palette so that the colors blend in the middle, but don't completely mix.

3 Press the Angel Wing bristles down on the palette and twist back and forth to splay them out.

4 Tip back and forth on the edge of your bristles to gently add dark and light colors to your surface. Roll back on the dark edge for dark areas and roll up on the light edge for the lightest areas.

DABBING

Hold a Petal (filbert tongue) brush perpendicular to the surface and make short, stabbing strokes to the surface.

STIPPLING

Use Diane's Angel Mist brush. Dip into paint and pounce out on your palette. Lightly touch down on the surface in a tapping motion. Every time you add a color, use less color and less pressure.

FURNITURE FINISHING TECHNIQUES

I approach the painting of furniture a little differently than I would if I were painting a small piece of tin or wood. There is much more surface to consider. Keeping your design simple will be to your advantage. Scroll work or vines are often used to connect design elements. Using faux finishing glazes with neutral and muted colors is a good idea to fill large areas of blank space.

I think it is very important to look through catalogues and magazines to get ideas for filling in the areas around your designs. Make yourself familiar with many styles of faux finishes. Everything should look very sheer and undefined so as not to distract from your design.

There is another way to use the glazes. Paint a very neutral color glaze onto the surface of your piece of furniture and then use various tools to create a design in the glaze. Practice on a piece of poster board first. You could use a splatter of alcohol, or a rake brush to create a plaid effect. There are so many things to experiment with. There is no end to the things you can do.

I have listed just a few techniques here which can and should be used when painting furniture.

Faux Finishing

If I am not painting a landscape, I love to use faux finishes as the background for the design. Apply the paint with a sea sponge to make color variations for a simple finish.

The sea sponge already has irregular holes in it and is round, so you won't get patterns of color that are too even. Always pre-wet your sponge before using.

There are many ways to faux finish. Try applying the paint with feathers, rags, doilies, paper towels and other interesting textures to get the right effect. Just using your fingers or the edge of your palm creates a great texture over wet paint.

When you transfer your design to the surface, trace as few lines as possible. Your pattern won't be as confusing to follow, and your painting will look more natural.

Spattering

1. To spatter, varnish the piece first so that you can wipe unwanted spatters away easily.

2. Thin the paint slightly with water.

3. Fill an Angel Wing brush completely with paint and gently tap the brush ferrule with another brush. Make a few test spatters on paper before you do the entire piece.

You can also use a toothbrush loaded with paint, then scrape a palette knife over it to create spatters.

Gold Leafing

Gold leafing is simple to do. It's just a little messy. You will need gold leaf, gold leaf adhesive, matte spray and acrylic antiquing gel.

Antiquing

1. Always varnish the piece before applying antiquing. This will keep the antiquing medium from going so deeply into the grain of the wood that you can't rub it out.

2. Apply antiquing medium to the surface and wipe the excess off until you are satisfied with the color.

3. Varnish when dry. Antiquing medium is also great for applying floated color.

Varnishing

There are many ways to varnish. A matte spray is nice for some projects, but generally a brush-on varnish covers better and more quickly. I use J.W. etc. Right-Step Satin Varnish, applied with a ¾-inch (19mm) glazing brush. Between coats of varnish, gently resand the piece and wipe with a tack cloth.

Lingerie Chest
with Roses

Unpainted Chest

I REPEATED THE DESIGN ON ALL OF THE DRAW-ERS OF THIS LITTLE CHEST TO KEEP THE DESIGN AREA FROM BECOMING TOO BUSY. HOWEVER, YOU MIGHT WANT TO PLACE DIFFERENT DESIGNS ON EACH DRAWER. ADDING THE STRIPES TO THE SIDES OF THE PIECE HELPS TO FILL LARGE EMPTY AREAS QUICKLY. THIS LITTLE CHEST IS SMALL ENOUGH TO FIT IN A SMALL BATHROOM OR BEDROOM. REMEMBER TO KEEP THE PAINTING LOOSE AND LIGHT FOR AN IMPRESSIONISTIC LOOK.

This full-size pattern
may be hand-traced
or photocopied for
personal use only.

SURFACE

This chest may be purchased from The Tole Bridge. (See Resources, page 126.)

BRUSHES

Eagle Brand Brushes, 710 Millennium series ⅜-inch (10mm) angle and ½-inch (12mm) angle, 715 Millennium series no. 12 flat, 770 Millennium series ¾-inch (19mm) glaze

DIANE TRIERWEILER'S SIGNATURE BRUSHES

Petal brush set (nos. 2, 4, and 8 filbert tongues), 10/0 striper

ADDITIONAL SUPPLIES

Masking tape or painter's tape, J.W. etc. Wood Filler, fine sanding disc, J.W. etc. Wood Sealer, tracing paper and pencil, water tub, Loew-Cornell Chacopaper, stylus, J.W. etc. Right Step Satin Varnish

PAINT: DecoArt Americana

Antique Rose

Avocado

Deep Burgundy

Evergreen

Light Buttermilk

Marigold

Olive Green

Pineapple

Sapphire

Uniform Blue

Buttercream
(Americana Satins)

Soft White
(Americana Satins)

PREPARATION

1) Fill, sand and seal the entire wood piece. Paint the entire chest with Soft White satin paint. This may take two or three coats. *2)* Use masking tape or painter's tape to tape off stripes on the sides of the chest and a border around the edge of the drawers. Paint these accents with Buttercream satin paint. *3)* Apply the pattern to the drawers.

Roses and Ribbons

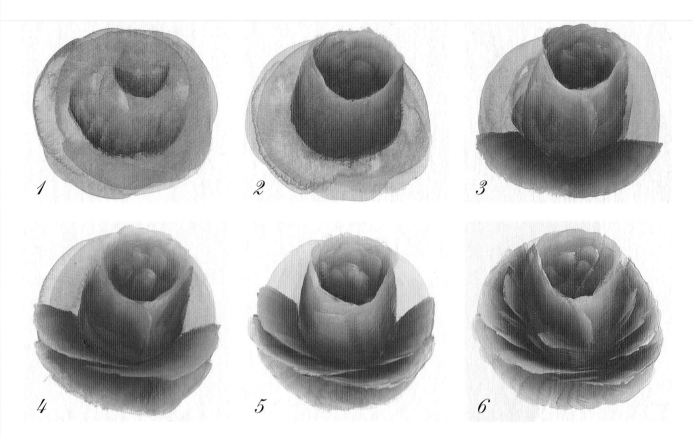

BUILDING A ROSE 1) Wash in a ball shape. Add shading with floats of color. Use a double-loaded brush to start the back of the rose cup. 2) Use a U-stroke to finish the front of the rose bowl. Add a few small petals inside. 3) Paint the bottom petal with a watermelon slice-shaped stroke. 4) Paint more petals, alternating them between the left and right sides. 5) Continue painting the side petals. 6) Add highlights to the edges.

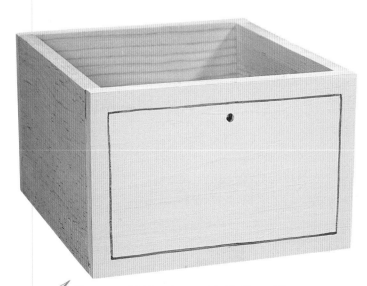

1 Use your 10/0 striper with Uniform Blue to create an outline between the border and the design surface on your drawer face.

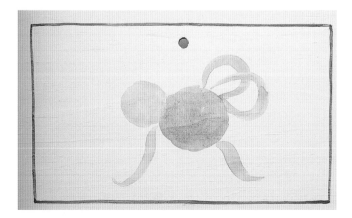

2 Use your no. 8 Petal brush, and wash in a ball of Marigold + water (1:1) for the yellow rose. Make a mix of Antique Rose and water (1:1), and wash in a ball for the pink rose with the same brush. Wash in the shape for the ribbon using your no. 8 Petal brush with Sapphire.

3 Use your ⅜-inch (10mm) angle brush with Antique Rose to shade in the cup and bowl of the yellow rose. Shade in the cup and bowl of the pink rose with your ½-inch (12mm) angle brush.

4 Use your ⅜-inch (10mm) angle brush and double load with Marigold and Pineapple. Stroke in the back petals in the bud area. Next, stroke in the front petals on the bud area. Paint the bottom petal of the rose in the shape of a watermelon slice. Work your way up the sides of the rose, alternating from one side to the other. Use the flat surface of your brush, work and pull to the chisel edge. Lightly buff the petals a bit while they are still wet.

5 Use your ½-inch (12mm) angle brush and double load into Deep Burgundy and Light Buttermilk. Paint the pink rose over part of the yellow rose to overlap the two roses. Paint in the same method as you did for the yellow rose.

6 Use your ½-inch (12mm) angle brush and corner load into Uniform Blue. Shade the ribbon where it crosses over itself and where it comes out from under the roses.

Leaves

1

2

3

4

5

BUILDING A LEAF

1) Base the leaf with a wash. Lay in the shading color using a No. 8 Petal brush. 2) Pull out strokes of shading with the petal brush. 3) Use the same brush to pull in highlight strokes. 4) While still wet, pull strokes of shading color into the highlight areas. 5) Paint the veins with thinned paint using a 10/0 striper brush.

7 With your no. 8 Petal brush, add water to Avocado (4:1). Fill in the leaves with this mix, and make the leaf edges a little uneven.

8 Add water to a mixture of Marigold and Antique Rose. Gently wash into the cup and bowl of the rose to re-establish the shade areas. Use your ⅜-inch (10mm) angle brush to re-highlight the edges of the petals with Pineapple. Next, use your ½-inch (12mm) angle brush to corner load into Pineapple and highlight the edges of the petals on the pink rose. Hit and miss this highlight to loosen the shape of the rose. This also ties the two roses together in color.

9 Use your ⅜-inch (10mm) angle brush and corner load into Evergreen. Shade the leaves through the center, at the base and along the bottom.

10 Give your leaves a little sunshine by corner loading your ⅜-inch (10mm) angle brush with Olive Green in the highlight areas. Then, use your 10/0 striper and Evergreen to place in vein lines. Be sure to follow the contour of the leaf when placing in vein lines.

11 Place filler leaves in with a mixture of Sapphire and Evergreen (2:1) using your no. 8 Petal brush. Loosely place in shadow leaves around the design.

12 Use your no. 8 Petal brush and Avocado to wash in a very light green around your design in the negative areas.

13 When the project is finished, paint the knobs and attach them to the drawers. Seal the entire piece with several coats of satin varnish.

Cherries on Ice-Cream Parlor
Stool

Unpainted Stool

LOOKING THROUGH STORES THAT CARRY PAINTED FURNITURE, I REALIZED THAT MANY TIMES THE COUNTRY FRENCH STYLE OF FURNITURE HAS FRUIT PAINTED ON IT. THIS ALSO GOES ALONG WITH THE 1950S STYLE OF FURNITURE THAT IS POPULAR NOW. THIS LITTLE ICE-CREAM PARLOR STOOL WITH BRIGHT RED CHERRIES ON IT WOULD BE NICE IN ANYONE'S KITCHEN.

Pattern

This full-size pattern may be
hand-traced or photocopied for
personal use only.

SURFACE

This was a flea market find but you shouldn't have any problem finding a piece that is close to the one in this project. You may find one of the stools at your local garage sales.

BRUSHES

Eagle Brand Brushes, 710 Millennium series ½-inch (12mm) angle, 700 Millennium series ¾-inch (19mm) flat and 2-inch (51mm) flat, 770 Millennium series ¾-inch (19mm) glaze

DIANE TRIERWEILER'S SIGNATURE BRUSHES

10/0 striper, Petal brush set (nos. 2, 4, and 8 filbert tongues), ½-inch (12mm) Petal brush, ⅜-inch (10mm) Angel Hair (rake)

ADDITIONAL SUPPLIES

J.W. etc. Wood Filler, fine sanding disc, J. W. etc. Wood Sealer, tracing paper and pencil, Loew-Cornell Chacopaper, stylus, water tub, J. W. Etc. Right-Step Satin Varnish, DecoArt Americana faux glazing medium, Decoart Americana matte spray sealer, masking tape or painter's tape

PAINT: DECOART AMERICANA

Antique Rose

Burnt Umber

Cadmium Red

Deep Burgundy

Evergreen

Light Avocado

Light Buttermilk

Marigold

Mocha

Olive Green

Titanium White

Violet Haze

Evening Blue
(Americana Satins)

Soft White
(Americana Satins)

PREPARATION

1) Most of these old ice-cream stools are a little damaged on the top surface, but the wood underneath is usually still nice. I peeled the top layer of wood skin off before I proceeded. *2)* Fill, sand and seal the wood. *3)* Base in the wood top and the metal edge with Soft White satin. *4)* Base in the legs with Evening Blue satin and a ¾-inch (19mm) glazing brush.

Checkerboard Trim

1 Tape the sides of the seat off lengthwise. Paint in the checks with Evening Blue satin. Let dry, and tape off the edge in the opposite direction. Paint in the remaining checks.

2 Pull up the tape and check for any leakage under it. Touch up if necessary.

3 Base the top edge of the stool in Deep Burgundy with the ¾-inch (19mm) flat brush. After you have traced the pattern, place it onto the surface.

4 Double load your no. 8 Petal brush into Mocha and Burnt Umber, and blend it out on the palette.

7 Shade the leaves with your no. 8 Petal brush loaded with Evergreen. The highlight color is Olive Green. Use straight paint to do this. Following the direction of the leaf, pull Evergreen through the center, at the base and along the bottom of the leaf. Use Olive Green to pull the highlights onto the leaves. It is not necessary to rinse the brush before you add another color; simply wipe it out on your paper towel. Sometimes you will need to use the flat of your brush, and other times you will be using the chisel edge. Use your 10/0 striper with Olive Green and place in vein lines.

5 Paint the branches first. Use your no. 8 Petal brush and make a mixture of water and paint (1:1) to fill in the leaves and cherries. Fill the leaves in with Light Avocado. Fill the light cherries in with Antique Rose and the dark cherries with Deep Burgundy.

8 Use your no. 8 Petal brush and brush-mix Olive Green and Titanium White. Highlight the edges of the leaves to pop the leaves up as they overlap other leaves.

6 Use your ⅜-inch (10mm) Angel Hair brush, and add a little water to Titanium White. Begin pulling this color onto the light parts of the branch in a slightly curved motion. This will highlight the branch and simulate the grain of the wood. Add water to Burnt Umber and use your Angel Hair brush to pull color onto the dark parts of the branch in a slightly curved motion. This will further simulate wood grain.

9 Use your ½-inch (12mm) angle brush and corner-load into Deep Burgundy. Tint the edge of each leaf. This complements the leaf and brings the cherry color over to it. Use your 10/0 striper to mix Olive Green and a touch of Titanium White. Place in vein lines off center, just above the shade line. Then, follow the contour of the leaf for the rest of the lines. Use your no. 8 Petal brush and Violet Haze to add backlights to the dark areas of the leaves. Add a little of this color to the shadows on the branch.

10 Use your ½-inch (12mm) angle brush to corner load into Deep Burgundy. Shade the dark cherries with this color. Pick the brush up and coax the color along instead of trying to make a precise stroke. Place in a C-stroke where the stem comes out of the cherry. Shade the light cherries in the same manner using Antique Rose. Apply a second shading to the cherries if they still need to be darkened.

11 Using your ½-inch (12mm) angle brush, corner load Olive Green to add an unripe area to the light side of the cherries. Also add this color to the light side of the indentation where the stem comes out. Be very loose and free with your strokes. Use the same brush and cornerload into Violet Haze. Add a backlight to the dark side of the cherries.

12 Use your 10/0 striper with Light Buttermilk and add a glint of light to the highlight side of the cherries. While this is still wet, smudge it with your finger to blend it in a bit.

13 Use your no. 8 Petal brush, and add water to Violet Haze. Lightly stroke in one-stroke leaf shapes around the design. Leave the edges loose. Add water to Light Avocado and use your ½-inch (12mm) Petal brush to wash a pale green color around the whole design.

14 Use your 10/0 striper with Light Avocado, and paint in tendrils and stems of cherries. Highlight the light sides of the tendrils and stems with a line of Olive Green.

15 I antiqued the stool with a mix of Burnt Umber and faux glazing medium (1:2). Simply brush over the surface with a 2-inch (51mm) flat brush and then wipe off the excess. I did this around the Deep Burgundy band. I didn't antique the design area, but you may if you wish. To prevent a halo of brown color, take a wet brush or your finger and gently blend the color to soften.

16 Use a 2-inch (51mm) flat brush to antique the sides and top of the stool.

17 Take a minute to analyze your painting.

I used a float of Burnt Umber to deepen the shade on the bottom of the branches. I was careful not to lose the Violet Haze backlight. I shaded the stem where it comes out from under the leaves. Wherever a leaf is over another, I used the no. 8 Petal brush with Olive Green to re-highlight. I made sure that the shading of Evergreen between leaves was defined. It was a little difficult because the wood was rough, but I cleaned up the edges of the cherries. I rechecked the highlight glints and found that they needed to be perked up a bit. I lightened the vein lines with a little Titanium White + Olive Green. I used a wash of Marigold (1:4 water) on the light cherries and a similar wash of Cadmium Red on the dark cherries. This added warmth to the composition.

If the antique medium is too close to the design, use your ½-inch (12mm) Petal brush to slip-slap a little Light Buttermilk over the area.

18 When the project is finished, use several coats of satin varnish to seal.

Table with *Berries*

Unpainted Table

MY HUSBAND PICKED THIS LITTLE TABLE UP AT A GARAGE SALE. I JUST LOVED THE RAISED DESIGN ON THE FRONT OF IT. IT LOOKS LIKE IT CAME FROM THE 1920S OR 1930S. IT WOULD MAKE A NICE END TABLE WITH A LAMP ON IT. THAT IS WHY I PAINTED MY DESIGN AROUND THE EDGE INSTEAD OF IN THE MIDDLE. I USED DIFFERENT VALUES OF THE BASE COLOR IN DIFFERENT AREAS TO MAKE THE PIECE MORE INTERESTING.

Pattern

This pattern may be hand-traced or photocopied for personal use only. Enlarge at 188% to bring it up to full size.

SURFACE

This table was found at a garage sale but you can adapt the design to fit a piece you already have. I chose to paint the table with the soft Sage Green satin paint because this color is so popular right now.

BRUSHES

Eagle Brand Brushes, 710 Millennium series ⅜-inch (10mm) angle and ½-inch (12mm) angle, 770 Millennium series ¾-inch (19mm) glaze

DIANE TRIERWEILER'S SIGNATURE BRUSHES

10/0 striper, Petal brush set (nos. 2, 4, and 8 filbert tongues), ½-inch (12mm) Petal brush

ADDITIONAL SUPPLIES

J.W. etc. Wood Filler, fine sanding disc, J.W. etc. Wood Sealer, tracing paper and pencil, Loew-Cornell Chacopaper, stylus, water tub, J.W. Etc. Right-step Satin Varnish, inexpensive cotton swabs

PAINT: DecoArt Americana

Boysenberry Pink

Burnt Umber

Deep Burgundy

Evergreen

Light Avocado

Olive Green

Pansy Lavender

Red Violet

Titanium White

Violet Haze

Sage Green
(Americana Satins)

Soft White
(Americana Satins)

PREPARATION

1) This table was already painted when we found it, so I lightly sanded it and filled some of the larger cracks. Basecoat the legs and the sides of the table with Sage Green. *2)* Mix Soft White + Sage Green (2:1), and use your ¾-inch (19mm) glazing brush to base in the top, the under shelf, and some of the turns on the legs. I also used this mix to drybrush the raised design and the pull on the front of the drawer. *3)* Apply basic pattern lines.

Vine and Leaves

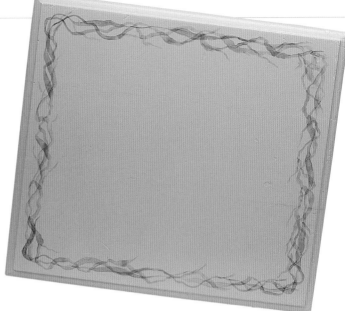

1 Use your no. 8 Petal brush and add water to Burnt Umber, making the Burnt Umber transparent. Pull your brush along on the flat and then on the chisel edge to create the shape of the vines.

2 Add three or four more intertwining vines.

3 Use your no. 8 Petal brush and double load into Evergreen and Light Avocado. Your paint should be a little creamy. Paint leaves in with a one-stroke method. Make sure you cluster the leaves. Vary the sizes by using less or more pressure on your brush. You may use a no. 4 Petal brush for smaller leaves. Technical note: It is important to use a wet palette when doing strokework. The water that flows up into the paint on the palette makes it easier to create loose strokes.

4 Use your 10/0 striper with Evergreen to create tendrils, connecting stems and vein lines for leaves.

5 To make your berries, use an inexpensive brand of cotton swabs. They have less fuzz in them. Dampen the swab in water and squeeze it out. Dip into Deep Burgundy and pounce out on your palette. Press your swab down on half of the pink berry. This will create the segment separations.

6 Dampen the other end of the cotton swab with water and squeeze it out. Dip into Boysenberry Pink and pounce out on your palette. Press your swab down on the other half of the berry.

8 Use your ½-inch (12mm) angle brush with Olive Green to highlight the ends of each leaf.

7 Paint the lavender berries in the same manner using Red Violet on one side of the berry and Pansy Lavender on the other side. Do not worry if the leaves are in the way of your berry placement. Just go right over them.

Berries, continued

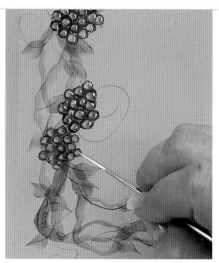

9 Use your ½-inch (12mm) angle brush with Red Violet to shade the lavender berries, and use Deep Burgundy to shade the pink berries. Shade around the edges to eliminate the open negative areas. Wash over the berries if there are too many open negative areas in the centers.

10 Use your ⅜-inch (10mm) angle brush to highlight with a float of Titanium White onto the left side of each berry. This is a C-stroke. Be sure to stay just inside of each berry segment, not along the outer edge.

11 Use your 10/0 striper with Titanium White to add a small glint of light onto each berry segment. This will be at about one o'clock.

12 Use your no. 4 Petal brush and double load into Evergreen and Olive Green. Blend out and paint one-stroke calyx leaves onto the berries—about five leaves for each berry. Use your 10/0 striper with Evergreen to paint connecting stems.

13 Add water to Violet Haze (4:1). Use your no. 8 Petal brush and paint one-stroke filler leaves around the design.

14 When your project is finished, use several coats of satin varnish to seal it.

Forget-Me-Not *Headboard*

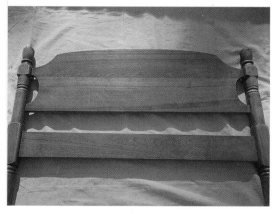

Unpainted Headboard

I AM FOREVER SEEING BED HEADBOARDS AT GARAGE SALES. IT MAKES YOU WONDER WHAT HAPPENED TO ALL OF THOSE FOOTBOARDS THAT GO WITH THEM. I STILL THINK JUST HAVING THE HEADBOARD ON A BED LOOKS FINE. I WANTED THIS PIECE TO LOOK A LITTLE VICTORIAN, SO I PAINTED SOME SCROLLWORK ON IT. IF YOU WANT IT TO LOOK PLAINER, JUST LEAVE THE SCROLLWORK OFF. LATER I FOUND THE LITTLE ROCKER, WHICH I PAINTED WITH A VARIATION ON THE FORGET-ME-NOT DESIGN.

Pattern

This pattern may be hand-traced or photocopied for personal use only. Enlarge first at 200% and then at 104% to bring it up to full size.

SURFACE

I found this old headboard at a garage sale. You might even have one in your own garage left over from one of the kids' rooms.

BRUSHES

Eagle Brand Brushes, 520 Azure series no. 6 filbert, 700 Millennium series 2-inch (51mm) flat, 770 Millennium series ¾-inch (19mm) glaze

DIANE TRIERWEILER'S SIGNATURE BRUSHES

10/0 striper, Petal brush set (nos. 2, 4, and 8 filbert tongues)

ADDITIONAL SUPPLIES

J.W. etc. Wood Filler, fine sanding disc, J.W. etc. Wood Sealer, tracing paper and pencil, Loew-Cornell Chacopaper, water tub, stylus, natural sea sponge, J.W. etc. Right Step Satin Varnish

PAINT: DecoArt Americana

Blue Chiffon	Burnt Sienna	Cadmium Yellow
Dioxazine Purple	Emperor's Gold (DecoArt Dazzling Metallics)	Hauser Medium Green
Napa Red	Olive Green	Primary Blue
Titanium White	Dark Ecru (Americana Satins)	Soft White (Americana Satins)

PREPARATION

1) Fill, sand and seal the wood if it doesn't already have a finish on it. Use your 2-inch (51mm) flat brush to base the entire piece with Soft White. *2)* Place the pattern on for the secondary color. Base this color in with Dark Ecru using your ¾-inch (19mm) glazing brush. *3)* Use your 10/0 striper with Emperor's Gold to line in the decorative scrollwork and to place in comma strokes and crosshatching. You may wish to freehand the forget-me-not design, or you can transfer on the pattern.

Forget-Me-Not

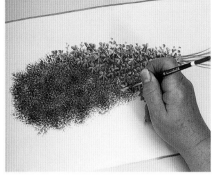

1 Use your sea sponge and Diox-azine Purple to create the general shape of the flower area. Sponge in a little Hauser Medium Green to create light and airy green shapes.

2 Paint stems with your 10/0 striper and Hauser Medium Green. Use Olive Green to line in next to the Hauser Medium Green for highlights. Use your sponge to dab in a little Primary Blue over the purple area and to bury the green stems. Use your no. 6 filbert brush and double load into Primary Blue and Blue Chiffon. Make a variety of one-stroke two-, three- and five-petal flowers. Keep them open and airy so that the colors underneath still show through.

3 Use a no. 4 Petal brush with a corner load of Titanium White to add lighter petals in the center area and on the top of some of the petals already placed. This will give a more rounded look to the bouquet.

4 Use your 10/0 striper and Hauser Medium Green to add stems in for ferns where the flowers are.

5 Use your no. 6 filbert and double load into Hauser Medium Green and Olive Green. Blend out and stroke on one-stroke leaves to create ferns coming out of the bouquet. Use your no. 4 Petal brush double-loaded with Primary Blue and Titanium White to add more petals on the outside edges of the bouquet. This will loosen up the design. Use Hauser Dark Green on your no. 4 Petal brush to add a few darker leaves on the ferns.

6 With your 10/0 striper and Hauser Medium Green, paint in tendrils.

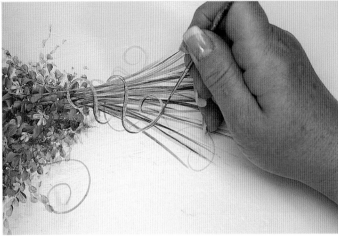

7 Use your 10/0 striper to paint in the centers of the flowers with Cadmium Yellow. Add a little line of Napa Red to the side of each center dot.

8 Load your 10/0 striper with Emperor's Gold to add a looping vine around the stems. Use Burnt Sienna and add a little hit-and-miss shadow line to the gold loop.

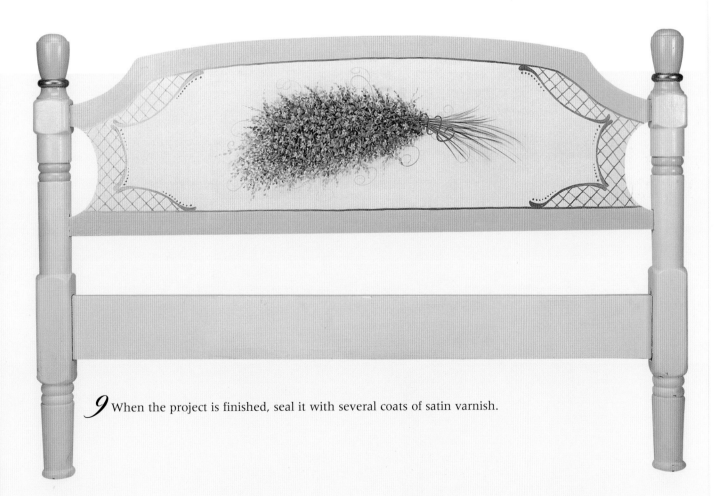

9 When the project is finished, seal it with several coats of satin varnish.

Secretary Desk
with Fruit

THIS LITTLE DESK IS ANOTHER GARAGE SALE FIND. AS YOU CAN TELL BY NOW, I GET A LOT OF PIECES FROM MY HUSBAND, WHO IS CONSTANTLY SEARCHING FOR THINGS FOR ME TO PAINT ON. IT ISN'T THAT HARD TO FIND NICE USED FURNITURE AT GARAGE SALES. YOU JUST NEED A LITTLE VISION.

I PAINTED THIS DESK IN YELLOW BECAUSE I THOUGHT IT WOULD SHOW OFF THE FRUIT BASKET WELL. THE NEW SHABBY CHIC OR COUNTRY FRENCH DÉCOR THAT WE SEE SO MUCH OF TODAY IS PAINTED WITH BRIGHT, VIVID SHADES OF BLUE, YELLOW AND GREEN. PLACING A STENCIL BORDER AROUND THE DESIGN CAN HELP FILL LARGE AREAS AND HELP FRAME THE DESIGN. FLYSPECKING AND ANTIQUING ALSO HELP FILL LARGE, EMPTY AREAS. FRUIT DESIGNS NEED NOT BE CONFINED TO JUST THE KITCHEN AREA OF THE HOME. THIS PIECE COULD BE USED IN ALMOST ANY ROOM IN THE HOUSE.

This pattern may be hand-traced or photocopied
for personal use only. Enlarge at 181% to bring it
up to full size.

SURFACE

This piece was found at a garage sale.

BRUSHES

Eagle Brand Brushes, 710 Millennium series ½-inch (12mm) angle and ⅝-inch (15mm) angle, 765 Millennium series no. 6 fan, 700 Millennium series 2-inch (51mm) flat; Delta ½-inch (12mm) stencil brush

DIANE TRIERWEILER'S SIGNATURE BRUSHES

Petal brush set (nos. 2, 4, and 8 filbert tongues), ½-inch (12mm) Petal brush, 10/0 striper

ADDITIONAL SUPPLIES

Black ultrafine Sharpie pen, DecoArt Matte Spray Varnish, Delta rope stencil (or pattern of choice), J.W. etc. Wood Filler, fine sanding disc, J. W. etc. Wood Sealer, tracing paper and pencil, Loew-Cornell Chacopaper, water tub, stylus, J.W. etc. Right Step Satin Varnish

PAINT: DECOART AMERICANA *(unless otherwise noted)*

 Avocado
 Berry Red
 Deep Teal

 Golden Straw
Light Buttermilk
 Royal Purple

 Sable Brown
Buttercream (Americana Satins)
 Emperor's Gold (DecoArt Dazzling Metallics)

 Stencil Cream Gold (Delta)

PREPARATION

1) Fill, sand and seal the wood piece. Use your 2-inch (51mm) flat brush to paint the entire piece with Buttercream. *2)* When dry, lightly spray the entire piece with matte spray varnish. *3)* Apply the basic pattern lines.

Fruit Basket

1 Use your ½-inch (12mm) Petal brush for the larger areas and the no. 8 Petal brush for the smaller areas. All design elements are based in with a wash of color: paint + water (1:2). Basket: Deep Teal. Pear and peach: Golden Straw. Cherries: Berry Red. Leaves: Avocado. Grapes: Royal Purple. Apple: Berry Red + Golden Straw.

2 Shade the leaves with a mix of Deep Teal + Avocado (1:1) on your ½-inch (12mm) angle brush. Shade the base of the leaves and the center vein line area. Corner-load your ½-inch (12mm) angle and shade around the outer edge of the cherries using Berry Red. Shade the grapes with Royal Purple. Use your ⅝-inch (15mm) angle brush to shade the basket using Deep Teal. Create the basket weave by shading with the ½-inch (12mm) angle brush and Deep Teal. Mix Golden Straw plus Berry Red and shade the pears. Shade the apples with Berry Red. When everything has been shaded once, shade once more in the darkest areas or in the corners using the same colors as for the first shading.

3 Use your no. 8 petal brush and wash Avocado into the negative space behind the cherries. Corner-load your ½-inch (12mm) angle with Berry Red and tint the edges of the leaves. Tint the cherries with Royal Purple and tint the grapes with Berry Red.

4 Use your 10/0 striper with Avocado to pull in tendrils around the design. Corner load your ⅝-inch (15mm) angle brush with Sable Brown and shade under the basket.

5 Use your no. 8 Petal brush with Emperor's Gold to drybrush here and there over the fruit and basket. Look over your entire design and make sure that you have brought your shadows out wide enough. Re-shade if necessary.

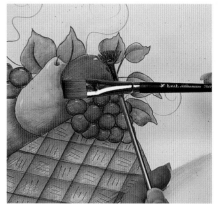

6 Begin lining around the design with a black Sharpie pen. Don't worry about staying exactly within the painted edges. It adds to the composition to have a little bit of the background color showing around the fruit. You may also choose to use a brown permanent ink pen for a softer look.

7 Use your 10/0 striper and Light Buttermilk to add highlight glints on all of the fruit.

8 Use your no. 6 fan brush with a little water in your paint to spatter the entire desk. I used Emperor's Gold. Place the paint in the fan brush and gently tap the fan with another brush. Test this procedure on your palette first. (See *spattering* on page 11.)

9 Use your Delta stencil brush with Gold stencil cream paint to apply a border around the front of the desk.

10 Be sure to use a light mist of matte spray varnish over your entire design before you brush varnish the piece. This will prevent the ink from smearing.

Floral Firescreen

EVEN IF YOU DON'T HAVE A FIREPLACE, YOU COULD PLACE THIS SCREEN IN A CORNER WITH A LARGE PLANT BEHIND IT. THERE ARE EIGHT BASIC FLOWER MOTIFS THAT YOU CAN USE TOGETHER OR SEPARATELY. FLOWERS AND HERBS PAINTED ON FURNITURE ARE VERY POPULAR RIGHT NOW, AND I THINK THEY ARE TIMELESS IN THEIR DESIGN.

Materials for Firescreen

SURFACE

This piece is a new piece of wood and can be purchased from The Tole Bridge. (See Resources on page 126.)

BRUSHES

Eagle Brand Brushes, 710 Millennium series ⅜-inch (10mm) angle & ½-inch (12mm) angle, 770 Millennium series ¾-inch (19mm) glaze, no. 6 filbert, 715 Millennium series nos. 10 & 14 flat and 2-inch (51mm) flat

DIANE TRIERWEILER'S SIGNATURE BRUSHES

10/0 striper, Petal brush set (nos. 2, 4, and 8 filbert tongues), ½-inch Petal brush

ADDITIONAL SUPPLIES

18 Kt. Gold Leaf Pen, J.W. etc. Wood Filler, fine sanding disc, J.W. etc. Wood Sealer, tracing paper and pencil, water tub, Loew-Cornell Chacopaper

Pattern & Colors for Roses

PAINT: DECOART AMERICANA

Burgundy Wine

Hauser Dark Green

Hauser Medium Green

Violet Haze

Light Buttermilk

Soft Sage

This pattern may be hand-traced or photocopied for personal use only. Enlarge at 181% to bring it up to full size.

PREPARATION

1) Fill, sand and seal the entire wood piece. Use your 2-inch (51mm) flat brush to base the entire piece with Light Buttermilk. *2)* Use masking tape to tape off the borders around the flower motifs. Use your ¾-inch (19mm) glazing brush to base the borders with Soft Sage. *3)* Transfer only the basic design.

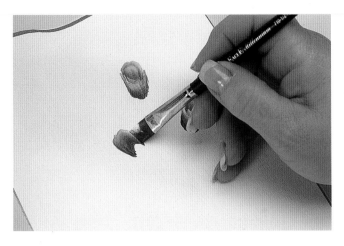

1 Double load your ½-inch (12mm) angle brush with Burgundy Wine and Light Buttermilk. Paint in the top **C**-stroke for the bud. Let dry and paint the stroke again.

2 Place a few small petals in front of the first petal.

3 Place another petal over the bottom part of your bud. Do this by double loading your brush and painting a **C**-stroke.

4 Stroke another petal in front of the bottom petal, dropping a little lower this time. Stroke over this petal twice.

5 Use your no. 4 Petal brush and double load with Hauser Dark Green and Hauser Light Green. Blend and place in one-stroke sepals at the base of each bud. Press your bristles down, and wiggle the brush as you come up.

6 Use your no. 4 Petal brush and double load with Hauser Dark Green and Hauser Light Green. Blend and use the chisel edge of your brush to pull on stems. Next, use your no. 8 Petal brush and double load with Hauser Dark Green and Hauser Light Green. Place on one-stroke leaves. Then, connect all the leaves to the main stem via the smaller stems.

7 Using your 10/0 striper with Evergreen, place on veins and tendrils.

8 Use your no. 8 Petal brush, and add water to Violet Haze. Make one-stroke filler leaves around the design.

9 Using your no. 8 Petal brush with Hauser Medium Green, wash behind the entire design. This will fill the negative areas and keep the design from looking as if it were a decal.

This full-size pattern may be hand-traced or photocopied for personal use only.

PAINT: DecoArt Americana

Black Plum

Burgundy Wine

Cadmium Yellow

Dioxazine Purple

Hauser Dark Green

Hauser Medium Green

Lilac

Olive Green

Pineapple

Royal Purple

Titanium White

Violet Haze

Leaves & Yellow Pansy

1 Base in your leaves with Hauser Medium Green using your no. 8 Petal brush. Pull your shadows on with Hauser Dark Green and pull your highlights on with Olive Green. Use your 10/0 striper with Olive Green + Titanium White to apply vein lines to leaves. (Refer to step by step demonstration on page 18.)

2 Corner load your ½-inch (12mm) angle brush with Burgundy Wine. Tint the edges of the leaves. Use your no. 4 Petal brush to basecoat the yellow pansy. Paint one petal at a time. Fill in the petal with Cadmium Yellow and while this is still wet, drag in Black Plum to fill in the dark areas.

3 Re-wet the lower petal with Cadmium Yellow and pull in Black Plum through the center. Continue to use your no. 4 Petal brush.

4 Corner load into Black Plum, and shade between the petals to separate them.

5 Use your 10/0 striper with Black Plum to add detail lines from the center of the flower pulling out onto the petals. Add a Burgundy Wine triangle in the center of the flower and let dry. Highlight the edges of the petals with a corner load of Pineapple on your ½-inch (12mm) angle brush. You may need to do this twice.

6 Use your 10/0 striper with Titanium White to make little comma strokes along the edge of the petals, above the throats.

7 Use your no. 4 Petal brush to fill in the pansy petals with Lilac. Start with the back petals first, finishing one at a time. Pick up a little Royal Purple on your brush, and pull shading into the wet Lilac paint. Continue with the rest of the petals. This will need to be done twice. Highlight the rounded middle part of each petal with Lilac.

8 Use your ½-inch (12mm) angle brush with a corner load of Dioxazine Purple to shade between the petals.

9 Use your 10/0 striper and Dioxazine Purple to pull the lines from the center of the flower. Add tiny lines of Cadmium Yellow just below the center of the flower. Base a triangular shape into the center of the flower with Burgundy Wine. Use your 10/0 striper and Titanium White to place two comma strokes near the center of the flower.

Mauve Pansies

10 Use your no. 4 Petal brush in a wet-on-wet method to paint the mauve-colored pansy. Do this with Burgundy Wine and Titanium White. Shade between the petals with your ½-inch (12mm) Petal brush loaded with Burgundy Wine. Load your no. 4 Petal brush with Titanium White and pull this highlight onto the edges of the petals.

11 Darken the center of the blossom with your 10/0 striper and Burgundy Wine.

12 Use your ½-inch (12mm) angle brush with Titanium White to re-highlight the edges of the petals.

13 Use your no. 8 Petal brush with Violet Haze to place the backlight color onto the leaves. Do this in the darker areas. Use the same brush to wash around the design with Hauser Medium Green. Use your 10/0 striper and Hauser Dark Green to place in tendrils and stems. Double load your no. 4 Petal brush with Hauser Dark Green and Olive Green, and place in a calyx at the bottom of the mauve blossom.

This full-size pattern may be hand-traced or photocopied for personal use only.

PAINT: DECOART AMERICANA

Burgundy Wine

Burnt Sienna

Cadmium Orange

Hauser Dark Green

Hauser Medium Green

Marigold

Olive Green

Pineapple

Violet Haze

Daisies

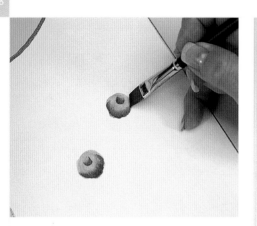

1 Use your no. 8 Petal brush and Marigold to base in the centers of the daisies. Use your ½-inch (12mm) angle brush and corner load with Burnt Sienna. Shade the center areas and the base of each center.

2 Use your no. 8 Petal brush and Marigold to paint one-stroke petals. Make sure that the petals are longer in the front and gradually shorter in the back of each flower.

3 Use your no. 8 Petal brush double loaded with Marigold and Pineapple. Add the next lighter layer of petals to the blossom and to the bud. Turn your brush onto the chisel edge to make smaller petals.

4 Use your ½-inch (12mm) angle brush with Burnt Sienna to float around the centers on top of the petals.

5 Use your ½-inch (12mm) angle brush and corner load into Cadmium Orange. Tint the edges of the petals in a hit-or-miss fashion. Make sure to add a little of this color to the tips of the back daisy to separate it from the front daisy. Also, tint the centers of the daisies and the bud. Use your 10/0 striper with Burnt Sienna, and pull little lines from the centers out onto the petals.

6 Use your no. 4 Petal brush with Pineapple to add a few more high-lights to the petals. Mix Hauser Dark Green and Burgundy Wine (1:1) to make a soft black. Dot in the seeds around the centers of the flowers with the tip of your 10/0 striper. Repeat with Pineapple and then with Cadmium Orange.

7 Use your no. 8 Petal brush, and double load into Hauser Medium Green and Olive Green. Blend out on your palette, and place in one-stroke leaves around the flowers. Use this same double-loaded brush on the chisel edge to place in some stems.

8 Use this same double load to add the calyx to the bud. Then, use your 10/0 striper with a mix of Pineapple and Olive Green to place vein lines on the leaves.

9 Add water to Hauser Medium Green and use your no. 8 Petal brush to add a subtle wash of color around the design. Using your 10/0 striper and Hauser Medium Green, add tendrils around the design. Add water to Violet Haze and tint around the centers and here and there on the petals. Next, use straight Violet Haze and your no. 8 Petal brush to add backlight to the darker areas of the leaves. Paint filler leaves with watery Violet Haze and your no. 8 Petal brush.

Pattern & Colors for Geraniums

This full-size pattern may be hand-traced or photocopied for personal use only.

PAINT: DecoArt Americana

Burgundy Wine

Cadmium Yellow

Hauser Dark Green

Hauser Medium Green

Olive Green

Titanium White

Violet Haze

1 Use your no. 14 flat brush and triple-load into Hauser Medium Green, Hauser Dark Green and Olive Green. Stroke on the leaves, keeping the light color on the outer edge and the darker color on the inside edge. You will need to stroke over the leaves twice to achieve the right color.

2 Use your no. 10 flat with Burgundy Wine plus a little water. Pounce on the chisel edge of the brush just inside of the outer edge of each leaf.

3 Load your no. 14 flat with Olive Green. Tap over the Burgundy Wine area to soften it a bit. I added another leaf to fill out the space better. Next, use your 10/0 striper with Olive Green to place in vein lines.

Florets

4 Use your no. 8 Petal brush with a wash of Hauser Medium Green and place this around the whole design. This is easier to accomplish before adding the pink florets. Use your 10/0 striper with Hauser Medium Green and then with Olive Green to place in the stems. Then, double-load your no. 6 filbert brush with Burgundy Wine and Titanium White. Create individual florets by using a one-stroke technique. Make sure the individual petals are not perfectly symmetrical.

5 Use your no. 2 Petal brush loaded with Cadmium Yellow to dot in the centers of each floret. You might need to do this twice. Then, using your 10/0 striper and Hauser Medium Green, connect the florets to the main stem.

6 Use your 10/0 striper with Hauser Medium Green to place on tendrils. Use your no. 6 filbert with Violet Haze to add filler petals.

This full-size pattern may be hand-traced or photocopied for personal use only.

PAINT: DECOART AMERICANA

Burgundy Wine

Hauser Medium Green

Olive Green

Royal Purple

Titanium White

Violet Haze

1 Using your no. 4 Angel Wing brush, double load with Burgundy Wine and Royal Purple and tap out on your palette. Tap lightly on the surface with the Burgundy Wine edge.

2 Flip the brush over and tap over the Burgundy Wine color with the Royal Purple edge. Add Titanium White to the Royal Purple edge, and tap out on your palette. Tap this color over the already formed flower.

3 Double load your no. 8 Petal brush with Hauser Medium Green and Olive Green. Blend out on your palette, and paint in a few one-stroke leaves around and in between the lilac blossoms. Add some stems with the chisel edge of your brush. To separate the lilac blossoms, corner load your no. 4 Angel Wing brush with Royal Purple and float between the blossoms. Keep this shadow loose and lacy. Then, using your no. 4 Angel Wing with Titanium White, stipple along the edges of the blossoms to get rid of any harsh edges.

4 Load your 10/0 striper with Hauser Medium Green, and paint tendrils and center vein lines on the leaves. Also connect some of the leaves with the stems. Use your no. 4 Petal brush and Violet Haze to add a little backlight to the darker edges of the leaves.

This full-size pattern may be hand-traced or photocopied for personal use only.

PAINT: DecoArt Americana

Burgundy Wine

Hauser Dark Green

Hauser Medium Green

Light Buttermilk

Limeade

Olive Green

Titanium White

Violet Haze

Lilies of the Valley

1 Paint one leaf at a time using your no. 8 Petal brush and Hauser Medium Green. While this is still wet, brush over the wet color with Hauser Dark Green.

2 Use the no. 8 Petal brush to add the highlight with Olive Green. Make sure to add this color while the leaf is still wet. Add Titanium White to the Olive Green for a second highlight.

3 Use the 10/0 striper with Limeade to place in stems for leaves. Base in flowers with your no. 2 Petal brush and Light Buttermilk.

4 Corner load your ⅜-inch (10mm) angle brush with Burgundy Wine. Shade the flowers lightly.

5 Wash around the design with Hauser Medium Green and your no. 8 Petal brush. Place tendrils in with Hauser Medium Green and your 10/0 striper. Then, use your no. 8 Petal brush with Violet Haze to place backlights on the leaves.

This full-size pattern may be hand-traced or photocopied for personal use only.

PAINT: DECOART AMERICANA

Burgundy Wine	Hauser Dark Green	Hauser Medium Green	Limeade	Marigold	Pineapple
Sapphire	Titanium White	Violet Haze			

Aster Blossoms

1 Use your no. 8 Petal brush loaded with Marigold to base in the flower centers. Then, corner-load your no. 8 Petal brush with Hauser Medium Green, and shade.

2 Double load your no. 4 Petal brush with Burgundy Wine and Titanium White. Stroke in the back, longer layer of petals first, and then add the shorter petals in the front.

3 Corner load your ½-inch (12mm) angle brush with Burgundy Wine, and float a shadow around the center of the pink flower. Double load your no. 4 Petal brush with Sapphire and Titanium White and stroke on the flower petals. These petals are longer than the petals for the other flower. Also, stroke on petals for a side view of the third flower. Place them in layer by layer to build up the fluffy nature of the flower. Use your ½-inch (12mm) angle brush loaded with Sapphire to shade around the center of the blue flower.

4 Use your no. 4 Petal brush and Titanium White to add more petals near the center of the flowers in order to add more dimension. Next, mix Burgundy Wine plus Hauser Dark Green (1:1), and use your 10/0 striper to add seeds around the flower centers. Repeat using Pineapple.

5 Double load your no. 8 Petal brush with Hauser Medium Green and Limeade. Blend on your palette and place in one-stroke leaves. Use the chisel edge of your brush to place in the stems.

6 Place in the vein lines with your 10/0 striper with Hauser Dark Green. Use Hauser Medium Green to place in the tendrils. Wash around the design with your no. 8 Petal brush and Hauser Medium Green. Then, add water to Violet Haze and use your no. 8 Petal brush to place in some filler leaves.

Pattern & Colors for Primroses

This pattern may be hand-traced or photocopied for personal use only. Enlarge at 111% to bring it up to full size.

PAINT: DECOART AMERICANA

Burgundy Wine

Hauser Medium
Green

Lilac

Limeade

Marigold

Royal Purple

Violet Haze

1 Double load your no. 6 filbert with Lilac and Royal Purple. Stroke on the flower petals for all nine blooms.

2 Using your no. 2 Petal brush with Lilac, pull your stroke from the middle of the bloom outward. Make sure to leave the center open.

3 Use your 10/0 striper with Royal Purple to create small detail lines, pulling from the center outward.

4 Use your ½-inch (12mm) angle brush corner loaded with Royal Purple to shade the bottoms of the centers where the petals attach.

5 Mix Marigold and Burgundy Wine together to make an orange color. Then, use your 10/0 striper to dot the seeds in around the centers.

Leaves

6 Use your no. 8 Petal brush, and double load with Hauser Medium Green and Limeade. Stroke on the leaves. Primrose leaves have scalloped edges, so push down on the flat of the brush and wiggle the brush back and forth while pulling toward the end of the leaf. You may need to stroke over the leaves twice for good coverage. Place in stems with the chisel edge of the brush.

7 Place in the tendrils with your 10/0 striper and Hauser Medium Green.

8 Use your 10/0 striper with Hauser Medium Green to place in vein lines on the leaves. Use your no. 8 Petal brush to wash around the design with Hauser Medium Green. Then, add water to Violet Haze and use your no. 8 Petal brush to place in one-stroke filler leaves. Use your Violet Haze to add backlights to the dark areas of the leaves.

9 When the project is finished, outline the screen and the inset panels
with the 18 Kt. Gold Leaf Pen. Seal the
piece with several coats of satin varnish.

Lawn Chair
with Morning Glories

Unpainted chair

YOU'LL SEE THESE OLD METAL CHAIRS JUST ABOUT EVERYWHERE. MANUFACTURERS ARE EVEN STARTING TO REPRODUCE THEM. I LOVE TO DECORATE MY GARDEN AREA TO LOOK LIKE AN ENGLISH GAR-DEN—ALL SORTS OF BIRDHOUSES, BIRDBATHS AND GARDEN ART. I THOUGHT I WOULD CARRY OUT THE BIRD THEME BY PAINTING A BIRD'S NEST ON THE CHAIR. AND WHAT COULD BE BETTER THAN SURROUNDING THE NEST WITH MORNING GLORIES?

These patterns may be hand-traced or photocopied for personal use only. Enlarge at 153% to bring them up to full size.

SURFACE

I picked up this chair at a garage sale. It is a 1950s-style metal chair and it should be easy to find either an old one or a reproduction.

BRUSHES

Eagle Brand Brushes, 710 Millennium series ½-inch (12mm) angle brush, 520 Azure series no. 6 filbert, 700 Millennium series 2-inch (51mm) flat brush, 770 Millennium series ¾-inch (19mm) glaze

DIANE TRIERWEILER'S SIGNATURE BRUSHES

Petal brush set (nos. 2, 4 and 8 filbert tongues), ½-inch (12mm) Petal brush, 10/0 Striper

ADDITIONAL SUPPLIES

DecoArt Americana's Faux Glazing Medium, paper and pencil, Loew-Cornell Chacopaper, water tub, stylus, J.W. etc. Right Step Satin Varnish, wire brush

PAINT: DECOART AMERICANA

Avocado

Burnt Umber

Evergreen

Golden Straw

Hauser Light Green

Light Buttermilk

Prussian Blue

Sapphire

Titanium White

Toffee

Violet Haze

Off-White House Paint

Uniform Blue

PREPARATION

1) Use a wire brush to remove any old flakes of rust and paint. Clean off dust particles with a damp rag. *2)* Use your 2-inch (51mm) flat brush to basecoat the seat and the back of the chair with Off-White house paint. *3)* Use your ¾-inch (19mm) glazing brush to base in the legs with Uniform Blue. Let dry, and place on the basic patterns.

Bird's Nest

2 Use your ½-inch (12mm) Petal brush and a wash of Burnt Umber to base in the bird's nest. When this is dry, corner load your Petal brush with Burnt Umber and shade in the center and the base of the bird's nest.

1 Lightly sand the chair where you are putting your design.

3 Use your no. 2 Petal brush and Burnt Umber to paint in the first layer of twigs.

4 Paint the next layer of twigs with Toffee using your 10/0 striper.

5 Use your no. 6 filbert to base in the three eggs. Do this with a mix of Sapphire and Light Buttermilk (1:10).

6 Using your no. 6 filbert, shade the eggs with a wet-on-wet method. Dampen each egg with the base color, shade with Sapphire and highlight with Light Buttermilk.

7 Use your 10/0 striper to add more twigs over the front of the eggs and along the sides of the nest with Burnt Umber and Toffee. This will make them look as though they are nestled inside of the nest. With your ½-inch (12 mm) Petal brush, corner load into Burnt Umber and float in the shading on the back wall of the nest, behind the eggs, and along the front edge of the nest.

8 Using your ½-inch (12mm) Petal brush, add water to Burnt Umber to place in a cast shadow underneath the nest. Tint the bottom of the nest and the cast shadow area with a wash of Violet Haze. Lightly tint the eggs with Violet Haze.

Morning Glories

9 Mix Avocado and faux glazing medium (4:1). Then, use your ½-inch (12mm) Petal brush and slip-slap on a subtle green background where the morning glory vine will be. Paint the vine with a mix of Burnt Umber + Avocado (1:1). Start at the bottom of the vine with your 10/0 striper, and vary the pressure on your brush to create the vine.

10 Double load Hauser Light Green and Avocado onto your no. 8 Petal brush. Paint heart-shaped one-stroke leaves up the vines. Place the smaller leaves on with the same colors using water mixed into the green and less pressure on the brush. Paint in the stems with your 10/0 striper loaded with Avocado.

11 Basecoat the flowers with Light Buttermilk using your no. 8 Petal brush.

12 Basecoat the flowers again with a mix of Sapphire + Light Buttermilk (1:2) using your no. 8 Petal brush.

13 Corner load your ½-inch (12mm) angle brush with Sapphire. Apply the first shadow to the flowers. Then, highlight the centers of the flowers with a float of Titanium White.

14 Corner load your ½-inch (12mm) angle brush with Prussian Blue, and apply a second shadow to the flower edges. Next, corner load your ½-inch (12mm) angle brush into Golden Straw, and shade the throats of the flowers. Use a little Prussian Blue to shade the eggs a second time.

15 Corner load your ½-inch (12mm) angle brush with Prussian Blue. Blend it on your palette and lightly apply ribs to the flowers. Use your 10/0 striper with Avocado to add stamens to the centers of the flowers.

16 Add tendrils with your 10/0 striper and Avocado. Use Evergreen to add the vein lines to the leaves.

17 Add water to Violet Haze, and use your no. 8 Petal brush to add filler leaves around the flowers. Then, corner load the no. 8 Petal brush with Violet Haze. Tint the edges of the flowers and add backlights to the leaves. Load your no. 2 Petal brush with Avocado, and add the calyxes to the flowers.

18 When the project is finished, seal it with several coats of exterior-grade satin varnish.

Chest
with Floral Garland

Unpainted Chest

I WANTED TO PAINT THIS PIECE AS IF IT WERE ONE LARGE AREA INSTEAD OF SEVERAL SEPARATE DRAWERS. I THINK THIS ADDED MORE INTEREST TO THE DESIGN. TO GET THE FEEL FOR THE SWAG DESIGN, I TOOK A GARLAND OF FLOWERS AND RIBBONS AND HUNG THEM ON TWO PEGS. SOMETHING AS SIMPLE AS THIS CAN INSPIRE A DESIGN.

This pattern may be
hand-traced or photo-
copied for personal use
only. Enlarge at 125%
to bring it up to full size.

SURFACE

We found this piece of furniture at a flea market but you could just as easily buy one at an unfinished furniture store.

BRUSHES

Eagle Brand Brushes, no. 710 Millennium series ½-inch (12mm) angle & ⅝-inch (15mm) angle, 770 Millennium series ¾-inch (19mm) glaze & no. 10 flat, 700 Millennium series 2-inch (51mm) flat, 520 Azure series no. 6 filbert

DIANE TRIERWEILER'S SIGNATURE BRUSHES

10/0 Striper, ½-inch (12mm) Petal brush, Petal Brush Set (nos. 2, 4, and 8 filbert tongues), ½-inch (12mm) Angel Wing

ADDITIONAL SUPPLIES

J.W. etc. Wood Filler, fine sanding disc, J.W. etc. Wood Sealer, tracing paper and pencil, Loew-Cornell Chacopaper, water tub, stylus, J.W. etc. Satin Varnish, DecoArt Americana Faux Glazing Medium

PAINT: DecoArt Americana

Blue Mist

Brandy Wine

Burnt Sienna

Burnt Umber

Hauser Medium Green

Hi-Lite Flesh

Limeade

Moon Yellow

Pineapple

Titanium White

Violet Haze

Beige (House Paint)

PREPARATION

1) Fill, sand and seal the entire wood piece. *2)* Base the entire wood piece using your 2-inch (51mm) flat brush with any beige house paint. I prefer a satin paint. *3)* Transfer on basic pattern or free-hand the design.

Basic Garland Shape

1 Use your ½-inch (12mm) Petal brush to scumble in colors where the garland shape will be. Start with Hauser Medium Green + faux glazing medium (4:1). The glazing medium will keep your paint from running when painting an upright piece of furniture and also will give you a more transparent effect. Repeat with Brandy Wine + faux glazing medium to simulate the background shadows of the flowers that will later be placed on.

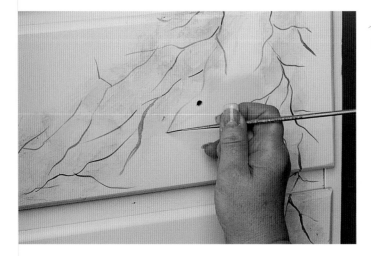

2 Use your 10/0 striper with Burnt Umber + water to place in the twigs.

3 Mix faux glazing medium to paint (4:1). Apply one-stroke leaves using a no. 8 Petal brush double loaded with Limeade and Hauser Medium Green. Cluster some of the leaves, and face them in all directions.

4 Use your 10/0 striper with Hauser Medium Green to place in the stems and the tendrils. Add water to Violet Haze and use your no. 8 Petal brush to place in filler leaves.

5 Load your no. 10 flat brush with faux glazing medium + Blue Mist. Stroke on the ribbons using the chisel and the flat of your brush. Highlight the ribbons with a corner load of Titanium White on the no. 10 flat.

6 Use your no. 8 Petal brush with Moon Yellow to base in the centers of the flowers. This will give you the location of the flowers. Double load your no. 6 filbert into Hi-Lite Flesh and Brandy Wine. Blend out and stroke on petals for the flowers. Use two strokes to create one petal, keeping the dark edge on the outside of the petal. Next, using your no. 6 filbert with Titanium White, pull this color from the center of the flower out onto the petal. This will highlight each petal.

7 Use your ½-inch (12mm) angle brush and corner load into Burnt Sienna to shade the flower centers. Use your 10/0 striper with Brandy Wine, and pull vein lines onto the flower petals. Dot in seeds around the centers with your 10/0 striper and Brandy Wine. Repeat a layer of lighter seeds using Pineapple.

9 Add faux glazing medium to Blue Mist. Then use your no. 8 Petal brush to add filler leaves around the design.

8 Apply small blue flowers using a double load of Blue Mist and Titanium White. Use your no. 4 Angel Wing brush. Apply the blue first and then add the white.

10 Add faux glazing medium to Blue Mist. Then use your ⅝-inch (16mm) angle brush to add a light trim color to the top edge and bottom of the chest. When the project is finished, paint on several coats of satin varnish to seal.

Cabinet with Landscape

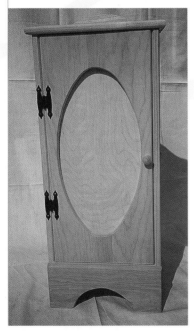

Unpainted Cabinet

I LOVE TO PAINT GARDEN LANDSCAPES. THERE ARE SO MANY WHITE ADIRONDACK CHAIRS PAINTED IN PICTURES THAT I DECIDED TO PAINT A BLUE ONE. IT MAKES A NICE CENTER OF ATTENTION. THE OVAL INSET PANEL IN THIS LITTLE CABINET IS REMOVABLE. YOU CAN FLIP IT OVER AND PAINT ANOTHER SCENE ON THE BACK IF YOU LIKE. I DIDN'T CARE FOR THE DARK HINGES ON THIS PIECE SO I REPLACED THEM WITH SMALLER BRASS ONES.

Pattern

This pattern may be hand-traced or photo-copied for personal use only. Enlarge at 200% and then again at 111% to bring it up to full size.

SURFACE

This wood cabinet can be purchased from The Tole Bridge (See Resources on page 126.)

BRUSHES

Eagle Brand Brushes, 710 Millennium series ⅜-inch (10mm) angle, 700 Taklon series 2-inch (51mm) flat, 770 Millennium series ¾-inch (19mm) glaze, 1550 Pure Red Sable series nos. 6 and 8

DIANE TRIERWEILER'S SIGNATURE BRUSHES

10/0 striper, Petal brush set (nos. 2, 4, and 8 filbert tongues), ½-inch (12mm) Petal brush, ⅜-inch (10mm) Angel Mist

ADDITIONAL SUPPLIES

DecoArt Americana Satin, J.W. Etc. White Lightning, fine sanding disc, J.W. etc. Satin Varnish, water tub, Loew-Cornell Chacopaper, stylus, graphite paper

PAINT: DECOART

Avocado

Burnt Umber

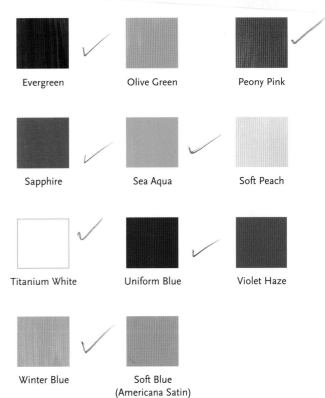

Evergreen

Olive Green

Peony Pink

Sapphire

Sea Aqua

Soft Peach

Titanium White

Uniform Blue

Violet Haze

Winter Blue

Soft Blue
(Americana Satin)

PREPARATION

1) Fill and sand the entire wood piece. Seal with J.W. etc. White Lightning. *2)* Use your 2-inch (51mm) flat brush to basecoat the cabinet with Soft Blue. Do not paint the inset panel. *3)* Base the edges of the oval and trim the wood with Emperor's Gold. *4)* Apply the pattern to the oval panel.

Sky and Trees

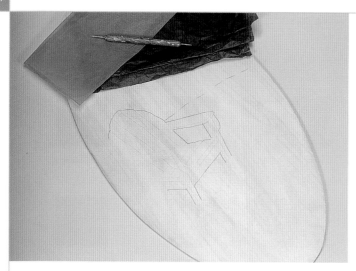

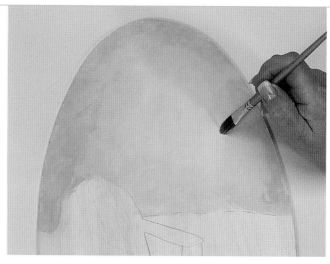

1 Transfer your pattern using both graphite paper and Chacopaper.

2 Use your no. 8 Petal brush and work with Winter Blue and Soft Peach to paint in the sky area. Scumble the colors on, making sure that the sky area is a darker value at the top, fading into light at the horizon line. There should be more of the peach color along the horizon. Be careful not to blend the colors into just one color. You should be able to see a little of both colors and a mix of the two.

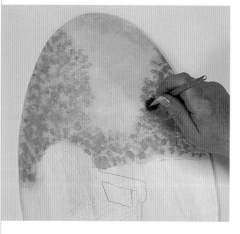

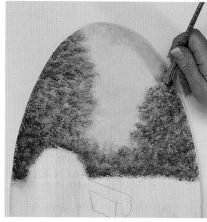

3 With your ½-inch (12mm) Petal brush, wash a tint of Peony Pink into the sky here and there. Use your ⅜-inch (10mm) Angel Mist brush with Violet Haze + water. Begin to stipple in the background trees with this wet color. This should be very light and subtle.

4 Using your ⅜-inch (10mm) Angel Mist, begin placing trees into the background area. Do this first with Evergreen, then with Avocado and finally with Olive Green. Work wet-on-wet. As you get closer to the horizon line, make sure the foliage is quite dense. For each successive color, use less pressure and less color.

5 Use the no. 4 Petal brush with Burnt Umber to place in the tree trunks and branches.

6 Use your no. 4 Petal brush with Violet Haze to place the backlights onto the trunks. Place this on the left side of the trunks on the left side of the composition and on the right side of the trunks on the right side of the composition.

7 Use your ⅜-inch (10mm) Angel Mist brush, and stipple a little Violet Haze back into the tree foliage. Stipple a little Sea Aqua, then Olive Green and then Olive Green + Titanium White (1:1) into the lightest areas of the foliage.

8 Use your ⅜-inch (10mm) Angel Mist brush to stipple in shrubs just above the grass line. Do this with Evergreen and then highlight with Olive Green.

9 To create the flowers in the background shrubs, double load your ⅜-inch (10mm) Angel Mist brush with Peony Pink and Titanium White. Tap out on your palette. Begin to stipple with Peony Pink and then add Titanium White over the wet pink. Repeat this method in other areas using Sapphire and Titanium White and Cadmium Yellow and Titanium White.

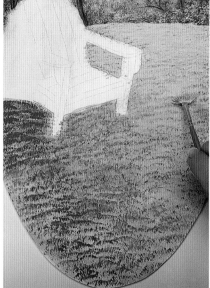

10 Using your ½-inch (12mm) Petal brush with Avocado, wash in a light color over the entire grass area. Load your ⅜-inch (10mm) Angel Mist brush and with Avocado and tap out on your palette. Begin to add blades of grass to the lawn area by lightly stippling. Do this over the entire area, adding more depth to the darkest areas.

11 Use your ⅜-inch (10mm) Angel Mist brush with Olive Green and stipple in lighter areas on the lawn. For the lightest areas, mix Soft Peach + Olive Green (1:1) and stipple in. Repeat again if necessary using Olive Green and Titanium White and re-highlight.

12 Using your ⅜-inch (10mm) Angel Mist brush, stipple in the foreground shrubs. Do this wet-on-wet using Evergreen and Olive Green. Then use your no. 8 Petal brush and wash in Evergreen to simulate a worn path in front of the chair.

13 Use your ⅜-inch (10mm) Angel Mist brush, and double load into Peony Pink and Titanium White. Tap out on your palette, and paint pink flowers in the flowerbeds using a wet-on-wet method. Stipple in the smaller flowers with Sea Aqua and Titanium White wet-on-wet. Use your no. 2 Petal brush with Cadmium Yellow and tap in a few oval shapes. Before this dries, touch these with Titanium White. Stipple in the darker flowers with the ⅜-inch (10mm) Angel Mist brush using Burgundy Wine and Titanium White in a wet-on-wet method.

14 Add flower stems using your 10/0 striper brush with Olive Green.

15 Use your no. 2 Petal brush with Uniform Blue to line in around the arms and frame of the chair.

16 With your no. 8 chisel blender, paint the boards on the chair using a wet-on-wet method. Use Uniform Blue in the dark areas and Winter Blue in the light areas. Paint one board at a time. Blend the colors together gently.

17 Use your no. 6 or no. 8 chisel blender with Soft Peach to drybrush highlights onto the lighter areas of the chair.

18 Reinforce highlights here and there with more Soft Peach and your no. 8 chisel blender.

19 Corner load your ⅜-inch (10mm) angle brush with Uniform Blue, and float between the boards to clarify the dark areas. Tint the chair with Sapphire to brighten it a bit.

20 Use your 10/0 striper with Uniform Blue to dab in little nail holes in the front face of the chair. Next, use Titanium White and your 10/0 striper to slash on a few bright highlights.

21 Using your no. 4 Petal brush with watered-down Uniform Blue, wash in cast shadows onto the chair. Apply additional shadows with Violet Haze.

22 Use a wet-on-wet method to apply base, shade and highlight colors to the pot. Use your no. 8 chisel blender to apply a base color of Soft Peach and gently blend in Burnt Sienna for the shadows. While the pot is still wet, apply Titanium White to highlight. When the pot is dry, brush a little Violet Haze for backlight in the shadow areas.

23 Use your ⅜-inch (10mm) Angel Mist brush to stipple Evergreen in the flowerpot. Repeat with Olive Green. Stipple in just a little Sea Aqua for the lightest value.

24 Double load your ⅜-inch (10mm) Angel Mist brush with Burgundy Wine and Peony Pink. Stipple the flowers in, first with Deep Burgundy and then with Peony Pink. Add a little Titanium White to your brush on the pink side and stipple in a lighter value.

26 With your 10/0 striper and Evergreen, place in taller grasses where the chair sits and throughout the flowerbeds. Pull in some lighter greens using Olive Green.

25 Using your no. 4 Petal brush and a mix of Sea Aqua and Olive Green (1:1), place in tiny one-stroke leaves around the blossoms.

27 Use your ⅜-inch (10mm) Angel Mist brush and a wet-on-wet method to add smaller filler flowers to the flower beds. Do this with Sapphire and Titanium White, Peony Pink and Titanium White, and Sea Aqua and Titanium White. Re-highlight any flowers that need to be lifted up with a stipple of Titanium White. Use your ½-inch (12mm) angle brush and Violet Haze to shade under the chair and on the right side of the grass area.

Wisteria *Screen*

Unpainted Screen

SINCE THIS PROJECT ENTAILED PAINTING ON SUCH A LARGE PIECE OF WOOD, I FILLED A LOT OF THE AREA WITH A FAUX FINISH. ALSO, SINCE DRESSING SCREENS ARE USUALLY PLACED IN A CORNER OR BEHIND A CHAIR, I PLACED THE BULK OF MY DESIGN TOWARD THE TOP OF THE PIECE. THE SHAPE OF THE PIECE REMINDED ME OF AN ARBOR, SO I FOUND THE IDEA OF THE TRAILING WISTERIA APPEALING. THE DESIGN IS QUITE SIMPLE TO PAINT AND COULD ALSO BE CARRIED OUT ON THE WALL NEXT TO WHERE THE PIECE WILL BE PLACED.

Pattern

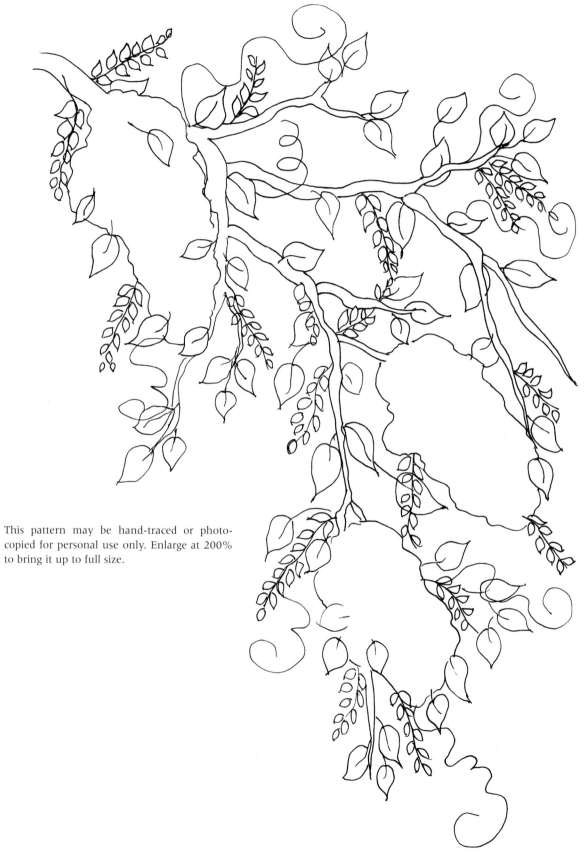

This pattern may be hand-traced or photo-copied for personal use only. Enlarge at 200% to bring it up to full size.

SURFACE

This surface can be purchased from The Tole Bridge (see Resources, page 126) or you may have your local woodcutter cut something similar.

BRUSHES

Eagle Brand Brushes, no. 720 Millennium no. 6 filbert, no. 720 Millennium no. 10 filbert, no. 770 Millennium ¼-inch (19mm) glaze, no. 700 Millennium 2-inch (51mm) flat

DIANE TRIERWEILER'S SIGNATURE BRUSHES

10/0 Striper, Petal brush set (nos. 2, 4, and 8 filbert tongues), no. 4 Angel Wing

ADDITIONAL SUPPLIES

Masking tape, 18 Kt. Gold Leaf Pen, DecoArt Matte spray, J.W. etc. Wood filler, DecoArt Americana faux glazing medium, fine sanding disc, J.W. etc. Wood Sealer, J.W. etc. Satin varnish, water tub, Loew-Cornell Chacopaper, stylus, tracing paper and pencil

PAINT: DECOART AMERICANA *(unless otherwise noted)*

Burgundy Wine

Burnt Umber

Emperor's Gold
(Dazzling Metallics)

Hauser Light Green

Hauser Medium Green

Royal Purple

Titanium White

Violet Haze

Warm Neutral

Off-White Latex Wall Paint

Swiss Coffee Latex Wall Paint

PREPARATION

1) Fill, sand and seal the wood. *2)* Use your 2-inch (51mm) brush to completely paint the wood with Swiss Coffee latex wall paint.

Applying the Faux Finish

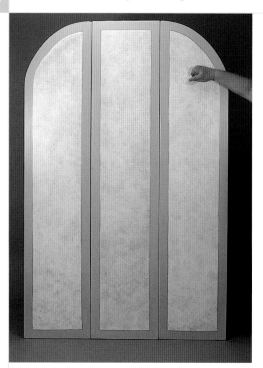

1 Make a mix of faux glazing medium and Warm Neutral (2:1). Scrunch up a piece of plastic wrap and dip into this mix. Tap out on your palette and apply over the entire wood piece. Use a mix of faux glazing medium to Emperor's Gold (2:2) and apply this very lightly over the previous step. Use the edge of your palm to touch over the surface to soften the colors together. Let this dry and tape off a two inch border around all the edges. Base this border in with a mix of Light Buttermilk and Warm Neutral (1:1). Use your no. 2 Petal brush with Emperor's Gold to apply a line between the border and the faux-finished area. You may also choose to use an 18 kt. Gold Leaf Pen.

Varnish the whole piece with a light spray of matte finish. In this way, potential mistakes can be wiped off easily.

Apply the pattern or paint the design freehand.

Laying in the Branches

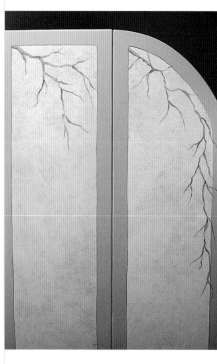
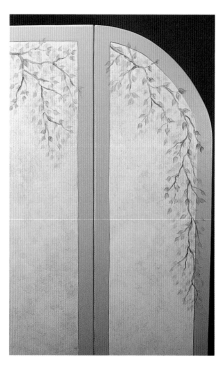

2 (Left) Use your no. 8 Petal brush with a mix of Hauser Medium Green + Burnt Umber (1:1) to place in woody vines. Use the chisel edge and flat of the brush.

3 (Right) Load your no. 10 filbert with faux glazing medium. Double load this into Hauser Medium Green and Hauser Light Green. Apply one-stroke leaves connected to the branches. For the smaller leaves, switch to your no. 8 Petal brush. Use your dirty brush and more glazing medium to scumble a light green haze around the leaves. Use your 10/0 striper with Hauser Medium Green to apply stems and vein lines. Use your no. 8 Petal brush with glazing medium and Violet Haze to place in the smaller filler leaves.

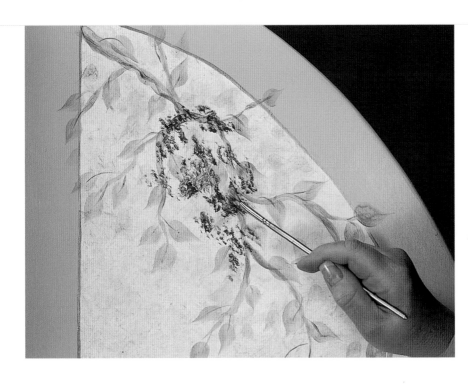

4 Begin to stipple in flowers with your no. 4 Angel Wing brush. Stipple with the corner of the brush. Do one flower at a time in a wet-on-wet method. Wet your brush with glazing medium and dip into Burgundy Wine. Stipple this in and repeat with Royal Purple.

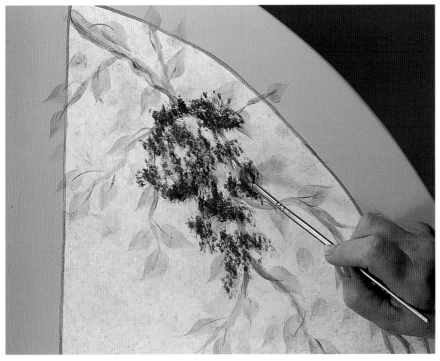

5 Next, stipple Titanium White over the wet Burgundy Wine and Royal Purple.

Purple Flowers

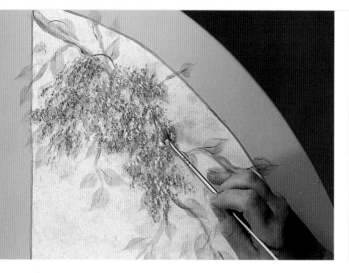

6 You can paint some of the blossoms with just two steps. Use Royal Purple and then Titanium White to stipple them in.

7 Use your no. 4 Angel Wing brush with Royal Purple to stipple a shadow area between the flowers. Rinse out your brush, and stipple along the light edge with Titanium White to break up the harsh edge of the shadow.

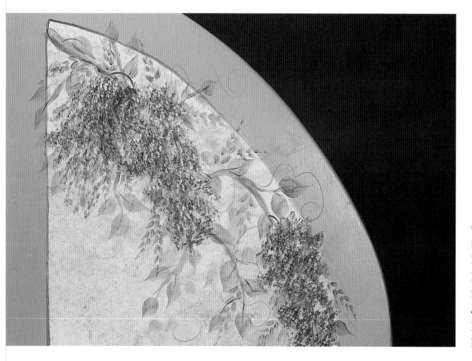

8 Mix glazing medium into your no. 6 filbert brush. Double load with Hauser Medium Green and Hauser Light Green. Place in one-stroke ferns. Then, use your 10/0 striper to apply tendrils, first painting with Hauser Medium Green and then highlighting with Hauser Light Green.

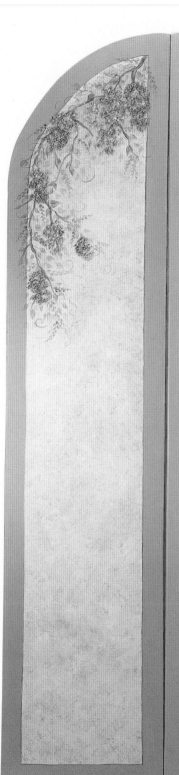

9 When you are finished, be sure to varnish the entire project with several coats of satin varnish.

Butterfly Hutch

Unpainted Hutch

THIS IS A SMALL, CHILD-SIZED HUTCH, BUT INSTEAD OF JUST USING THIS PIECE IN A CHILD'S ROOM, YOU MAY WANT TO USE IT ON YOUR PATIO OR SCREENED-IN PORCH. IT WOULD MAKE A GREAT CONVERSATION PIECE AND A PLACE TO STORE GARDEN TOOLS AND GADGETS. INSECTS LIKE BUTTERFLIES ARE VERY POPULAR RIGHT NOW. WHY NOT ADD A LITTLE BIT OF NATURE TO YOUR HOME?

Patterns

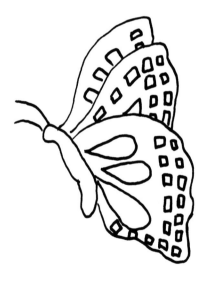

These full-size patterns may be hand-traced
or photocopied for personal use only.

SURFACE

This piece was purchased from a flea market. I am sure that you will find something wonderful to put the design on. Children's furniture is not too hard to find.

BRUSHES

Eagle Brand Brushes, 710 Millennium series ⅜-inch (10mm) angle, 770 Millennium series ¾-inch (19mm) glaze, 700 Millennium series ½-inch (12mm) flat

DIANE TRIERWEILER'S SIGNATURE BRUSHES

10/0 Striper, Petal brush set (nos. 2, 4, and 8 filbert tongues), ⅜-inch (10mm) Angel Hair

ADDITIONAL SUPPLIES

Masking tape, J.W. etc. Wood Filler, fine sanding disc, J.W. etc. First Step Wood Sealer, tracing paper and pencil, water tub, Loew-Cornell Chacopaper, black Sharpie pen, stylus, natural sea sponge, J.W. etc. Satin Varnish

PAINT: DecoArt Americana *(unless otherwise noted)*

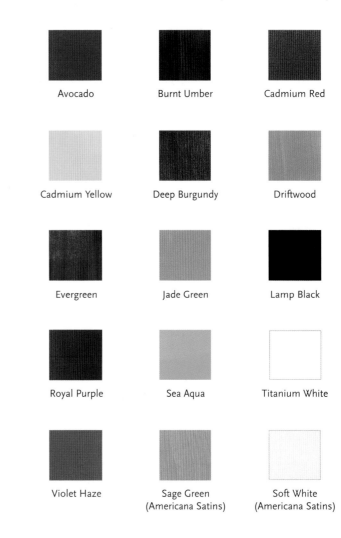

Avocado | Burnt Umber | Cadmium Red

Cadmium Yellow | Deep Burgundy | Driftwood

Evergreen | Jade Green | Lamp Black

Royal Purple | Sea Aqua | Titanium White

Violet Haze | Sage Green (Americana Satins) | Soft White (Americana Satins)

PREPARATION

1) This piece of furniture was already stained and varnished. It was very dark in color. I sanded it thoroughly and filled the bigger cracks. I like the character of distressed wood, so I didn't spend a lot of time refinishing. I used my ½-inch (12mm) flat brush to basecoat the whole piece with Soft White. *2)* When you have good coverage on your surface and it is dry, use masking tape to form striping behind the shelves. Use your sea sponge to tap in Sage Green to create stripes. This can look a little textured and airy. *3)* Base in the edges of the furniture piece with Sage Green satin. *4)* Apply the patterns.

Branch

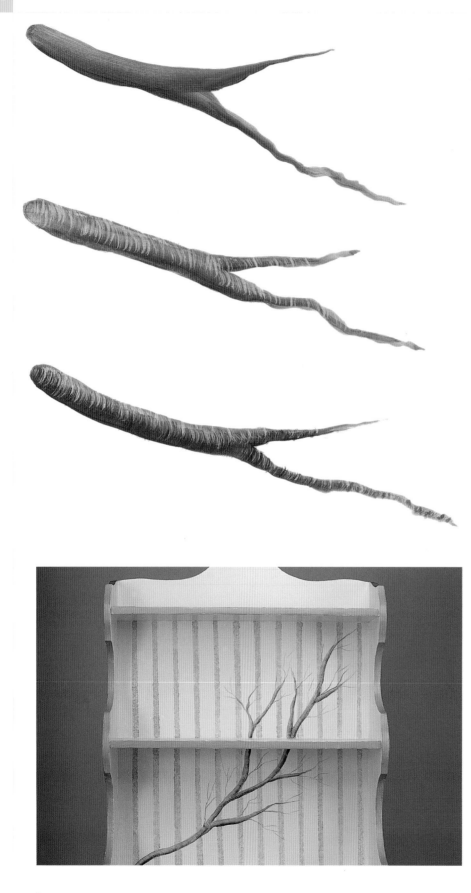

1 Double load your no. 8 Petal brush with Driftwood and Burnt Umber. Pull in a branch by using the chisel and the flat of your brush. Add smaller branches with your 10/0 striper and Burnt Umber. Use your ⅜-inch (10mm) Angel Hair brush and Titanium White to add highlights to the top edge of the branch. Repeat this method on the bottom of the branch with Burnt Umber to shade.

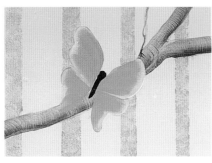

2 Use your no. 2 Petal brush to fill in the Moth body with Lamp Black. Then, use your no. 8 Petal brush to fill in the wings with Jade Green.

3 Corner-load your ⅜-inch (10mm) angle brush with Titanium White. Highlight the edges of the wings. Corner-load your ⅜-inch (10mm) angle brush with Sea Aqua and use the chisel edge of the brush to add striping lines.

4 Use the 10/0 striper brush with Royal Purple to add detail lines around the edge of the wings. Finish detailing the edge of the wings with Lamp Black. Add fine vein lines on the wings with Lamp Black. Next, place a Lamp Black dot on the wings. Outline this with Royal Purple. Add a small line next to the black dot with Cadmium Yellow. Highlight the body with a float of Titanium White on your ⅜-inch (10mm) angle brush.

5 Mix Cadmium Red + Cadmium Yellow (1:2). Use your no. 4 Petal brush to base in the wings of the orange butterfly. Then, use your no. 2 Petal brush to base in the body with Lamp Black.

6 Corner load your ⅜-inch (10mm) angle brush with Cadmium Red and shade the edges of the wings. Corner load with Cadmium Yellow and highlight the wings.

7 Use your 10/0 striper with Violet Haze to outline the bottoms of the wings. Use your 10/0 striper with Cadmium Yellow to add lines and large oval shapes to the wings.

Butterflies, continued

8 Base in the wings of the red butterfly with Cadmium Red using your no. 4 Petal brush. Then, base in the body with the no. 2 Petal brush and Lamp Black.

9 Corner load your ⅜-inch (10mm) angle brush into Cadmium Red, and shade the yellow areas on the wings.

10 Use your 10/0 striper with Royal Purple to pull some lines over the black areas on the wings.

11 Use your no. 4 Petal brush with Cadmium Yellow to base in the wings of the monarch butterfly. Use your no. 2 Petal brush with Lamp Black to base in the body and the black areas around the wings.

12 Use your ⅜-inch (10mm) angle to float a Deep Burgundy shade along the edges of all of the wings. Pull some of this color onto the wings. Highlight the edges of the wings with a float of Cadmium Yellow.

13 Using your 10/0 striper with Lamp Black, paint in the lines on the edges of the wings and on the body.

With your black Sharpie pen, make a whimsical little broken line behind the butterfly to simulate the trail of his flight path.

14 Add water to Avocado, and use your no. 8 Petal brush to paint in one-stroke leaves on and around the branches. Use your 10/0 striper with Evergreen to add vein lines to the leaves. Next, add water to Violet Haze and use your no. 8 Petal brush to add one-stroke filler leaves around the design. Drybrush a little Violet Haze into the darker areas of the branch. Then, using your no. 8 Petal brush, make a wash of Burnt Umber to place a shadow under the monarch butterfly.

When the piece has been completely painted, varnish with at least two coats of satin varnish.

Armoire
with Roses and Ribbons

Unpainted Armoire

IN KEEPING WITH THE COUNTRY FRENCH THEME I LIKE TO PAINT, I USED THE PASTEL YELLOW AND BLUE TONES THAT ARE POPULAR TODAY ON THIS OLD ARMOIRE. USING A FAUX FINISH ON THE DOORS AND CROWN MOULDING HELPED FILL A LOT OF THE EMPTY AREAS. THE TINY STRIPE BEHIND THE DESIGN GIVES THE SURFACE TEXTURE FOR THE DESIGN TO SIT ON. YOU COULD ALSO USE A STRIPED WALL COVERING AND APPLY THIS TO THE DOOR FRONTS. PAINTING OVER WALLPAPER IS FUN, AND THERE IS NO PREPARATION. YOU DO NEED TO BE MORE CAREFUL WITH YOUR PAINTING, SO I SUGGEST THAT YOU VARNISH OVER THE PAPER BEFORE YOU START PAINTING.

This pattern may be hand-traced or photocopied for personal use only. Enlarge at 181% to bring it up to full size.

SURFACE

I purchased this armoire at a local charity antique show. It is a great old piece to paint on. You may be able to find something similar at an unfinished furniture store. An armoire makes a great entertainment center or a storage place for linens.

BRUSHES

Eagle Brand Brushes, 715 Millennium series no. 14 flat, 710 Millennium series ½-inch (12mm) angle & ⅝-inch (15mm) angle, no. 720 Millennium no. 6 filbert, 700 Millennium series 2-inch (51mm) flat

DIANE TRIERWEILER'S SIGNATURE BRUSHES

10/0 striper, ½-inch (12mm) angel hair, ½-inch (12mm) Petal brush, no. 8 Petal brush (filbert tongue), no. 2 Angel Wing

ADDITIONAL SUPPLIES

DecoArt Americana Faux Glazing Medium, Plaid's Multipurpose Rubber Faux Striation Tool, wood filler, fine sanding disc, J.W. etc. First Step Wood Sealer, tracing paper and pencil, stylus, Loew-Cornell Chacopaper, water tub, J.W. etc. Right Step Satin Varnish

PAINT: DECOART AMERICANA *(unless otherwise noted)*

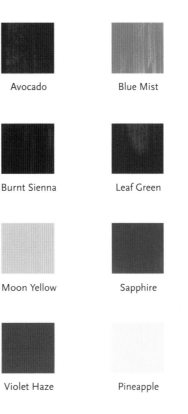

Avocado	Blue Mist	Burgundy Wine
Burnt Sienna	Leaf Green	Limeade
Moon Yellow	Sapphire	Titanium White
Violet Haze	Pineapple	White (House Paint)

PREPARATION

1) Fill, sand and seal the entire wood piece. *2)* Follow the step-by-step instructions on how to base and faux finish the wood in the following pages. *3)* Apply a loose pattern to doors or freehand the design.

Basecoat, Striations and Faux Finish

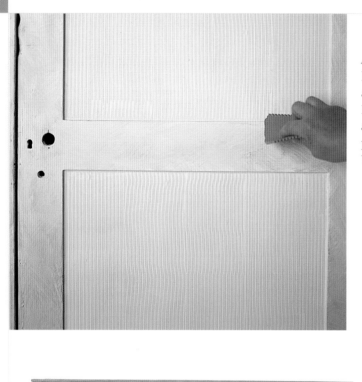

1 Basecoat the entire armoire in several coats of white house paint. The striation lines on the armoire were applied with a striation tool. You will need to mix one part Pineapple + faux glazing medium (1:6). Paint one panel at a time, using a large brush to apply the paint mix and then pulling the tool from the top to the bottom of each panel. Wipe the tool on a towel each time you pull down.

2 To create the blue accent faux finish, use glazing medium + Sapphire (6:1). With a 2-inch (51mm) flat brush, slip-slap the mixture sparingly onto the drawers, the crown molding and the trim on the doors. If the color becomes a little bright, you may want to add a little of the white house paint.

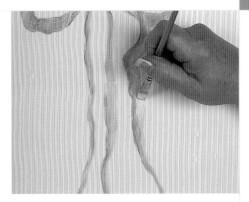

3 Basecoat the bow, using a no. 14 flat brush loaded with faux glazing medium and Sapphire. The color in your brush should be very light and transparent. Begin with the center of the knot on the chisel edge of the brush, and change to the flat of the brush to get variations in the size of the ribbon. The long, trailing ribbons should look like they are hanging behind the middle rail of the door. This will give you a trompe l'oeil effect. You will probably have to apply the paint twice—the first coat to place the design and the second coat to get the wider areas of the ribbon darker.

4 Highlight the curved areas of the ribbons and bow by drybrushing little bit of Titanium White on your ½-inch (12mm) Angel Hair brush. Use straight paint for this to get maximum brightness.

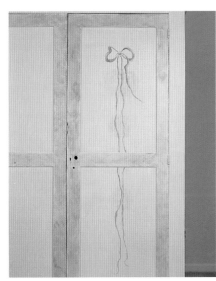

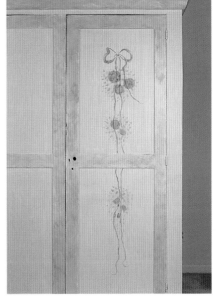

5 Use your ½-inch (12mm) Petal brush with Leaf Green + glazing medium. Slip-slap the color on to add background greens and to establish positioning of the design elements. The glazing medium will remain wet for a while, so if you wish to remove any of the paint, it will come off easily.

6 Use your ½-inch (12mm) Petal brush with glazing medium + Leaf Green to paint in a few one-stroke leaves. If the medium becomes a little sticky, add a little bit of water to your brush.

7 Block in the roses and rosebuds with your no. 8 Petal brush and glazing medium + Burgundy Wine. Continue to use the glazing medium for easy removal of the paint if necessary and for transparency in the design elements.

Detailing Ribbons and Roses

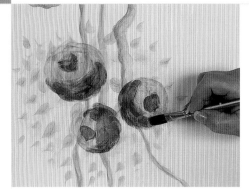

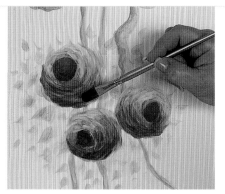

8 Corner load your ½-inch (12mm) Petal brush with Burgundy Wine. Shade in the cup and the bowl of the roses. Make sure the roses and buds are facing in different directions.

9 Use your ½-inch (12mm) Petal brush to shade and highlight the large roses and the no. 8 Petal brush for the smaller roses. Add glazing medium to your Burgundy Wine and then add a little Titanium White to this color. Begin to place in light rose petals on roses with a wet-on-wet technique. Work mostly on the chisel edge of the brush, and pull from the outer edge inward. The petals will get lighter on the light side of the roses and get darker on the dark side of the roses.

10 Use your dirty brush to slip-slap a bit of color around the roses. Layering colors like this will give your design more dimension. Return to your roses, and add another layer of highlight to the light side and more shadow to the dark side. Do this with the ½-inch (12mm) Petal brush for the large roses and the no. 8 Petal brush for the small roses. Add water to your paint, and wash on the colors.

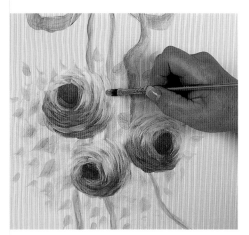

11 Make sure your roses are dry before you go on with the next layer of color. Add more petals to the roses, using Titanium White for the light side and Burgundy Wine for the dark side. Use your ½-inch (12mm) Petal or your no. 8 Petal brush.

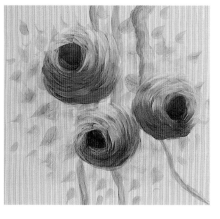

12 Use your ½-inch (12mm) Petal brush and Violet Haze to add back-lights to the bottom of each rose.

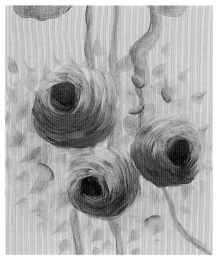

13 Use your no. 6 filbert brush with Moon Yellow to place in the centers to the flowers. This will help you locate where and how many flowers you will have in your design. Use your ½-inch (12mm) angle brush corner loaded into Burnt Sienna to shade the centers.

14 Double load your no. 6 filbert brush with Titanium White and Sapphire. Place petals on using the chisel edge of the brush with the light side up. Pull from the outside into the center. When this layer is dry, continue adding more shorter petals on top of the ones already there. Gradually use only the Titanium White.

15 Using your 10/0 striper, mix Leaf Green + Burgundy Wine (1:1) to create a soft black. Place in seeds around the centers of the flowers.

16 Base the centers to the daisies with Moon Yellow and your no. 8 Petal brush. Use your ½-inch (12mm) angle brush corner loaded with Burnt Sienna to shade the centers. Next, use your no. 8 Petal brush with Violet Haze to understroke the daisy petals. These are one-strokes, starting from the outside pulling into the centers.

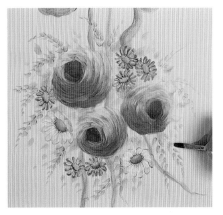

17 Use your no. 8 Petal brush with Titanium White to overstroke daisy petals. Make sure to leave a little of the underpetal still showing.

18 Use your no. 6 filbert with Titanium White to add another shorter layer of petals. These are also one-strokes. Double load your no. 8 Petal brush with Moon Yellow and Burnt Sienna and re-shade your centers. Then, using your 10/0 striper, mix together Leaf Green and Burgundy Wine (1:1) and place in the seeds around the centers.

19 Load your no. 8 Petal brush with glazing medium and Avocado. Place in some fernlike leaves coming out from the design. These are small one-strokes. Next, use your 10/0 striper with Avocado to place in stems connecting the fern leaves together. Also, place in tendrils with Avocado.

Leaves and Queen Anne's Lace

20 Using your no. 8 Petal brush with Limeade, base in each individual rose leaf. You may need to repeat this step in order to provide adequate coverage.

21 Use your no. 8 Petal brush with Leaf Green to begin placing in the dark values. Place in the vein line and the shadow areas. While this color is still wet, begin pulling the Limeade highlight onto the leaf in the other direction. Finish each leaf before you move on. You may need to place these colors in twice for good coverage. This method will help you make leaves that all look a little different and more impressionistic. (See page 18.)

22 Use your 10/0 striper brush with Leaf Green to apply vein lines. Then, using your no. 8 Petal brush with glazing medium and Leaf Green, place in small filler leaves.

23 Use your 10/0 striper with Leaf Green to place in connecting stems to the leaves and flowers. Then load your no. 2 Angel Wing brush with Blue Mist. This color will be the foundation for the Queen Anne's lace.

24 Use your no. 2 Angel Wing to stipple Titanium White over the Blue Mist on the Queen Anne's lace. Finish one flower at a time while it is still wet. Add glazing medium to the Blue Mist, and use your ½-inch (12mm) Petal brush to slip-slap this color in and around the design. Use your 10/0 striper with Avocado to place in the tendrils.

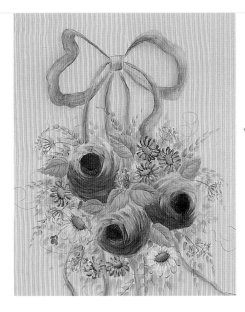

25 Load your no. 8 Petal brush with glazing medium and Violet Haze. Add a few filler leaves, using a one-stroke method. Next, mix a little Golden Straw with Burgundy Wine, and use your 10/0 striper to tap a few seed dots in the center of the roses. At first, I was going to paint the left side of the ribbon over the bouquet, but I changed my mind and decided to tuck it behind the flowers like the other ribbon. I used the no. 14 flat brush loaded with glazing medium and Sapphire to repair the ribbon. Then, I highlighted the ribbon with Titanium White.

26 Corner load your ⅝-inch (15mm) angle brush with a lot of water and Blue Mist. Shade next to the bows and ribbons on the left side, making this light and subtle—just a suggestion. This adds dimension to the piece and helps the design stand out from the background.

When the entire design has been painted, make sure to varnish with at least two coats of satin varnish.

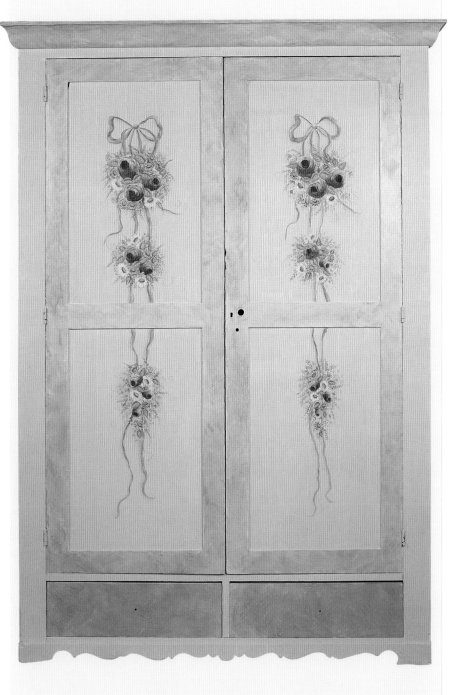

Resources

DecoArt Products
P.O. Box 360
Stanford, KY 40484
(800) 367-3047

Eagle Brand Brushes
2231 Robinson Rd. NE
Suite A
Marietta, GA 30068
(800) 832-4532

J.W. Etc.
2205 First Street, Suite 103
Simi Valley, CA 93065
(805) 526-5066

Loew-Cornell
563 Chestnut Avenue
Teaneck, NY 07666-2490
(201) 836-7070
www.loew-cornell.com

The Tole Bridge
1875 Norco Drive
Norco, CA 92860
(909) 272-6918
www.dianetrierweiler.com

Look for these other *fine decorative painting titles!*

Handpainting Your Furniture

Handpainting furniture is fun, inexpensive and—with this book—easy to do. These nine step-by-step projects feature an exciting array of realistic scenes and trompe l'oeil effects for decorating all kinds of furniture. Clear instructions leave nothing to chance and cover everything from preparing surfaces and scaling up drawings to techniques for giving each piece an authentic, antique look.

ISBN 0-89134-980-4, paperback, 128 pages, #31539-K

The Complete Book of Decorative Painting

Get the must-have one-stop reference for decorative painters, crafters, home decorators and do-it-yourselfers! This book is packed with solutions to every painting challenge, including surface preparation, lettering, borders, faux finishes, strokework techniques and more! You'll also find five complete fun-to-paint projects!

ISBN 1-58180-062-2, paperback, 256 pages, #31803-K

Color for the Decorative Painter

This guide makes using color simple. Best of all, it's as fun as it is instructional, featuring ten step-by-step projects that illustrate color principles in action. As you paint your favorite subjects, you'll learn how to make color work for you. No second-guessing, no regrets—just great-looking paintings and a whole lot of pleasure.

ISBN 1-58180-048-7, paperback, 128 pages, #31796-K

From Flea Market to Fabulous

Fantastic treasures await you, hidden among piles of junk at garage sales and swap meets. With this book, you'll learn how to transform those spectacular bargains into beautiful pieces of art and furniture. Ten gorgeous step-by-step projects make it easy, fast, and fun!

ISBN 1-58180-092-4, paperback, 144 pages, #31740-K

These books and other fine North Light titles are available from your local art & craft retailer, bookstore, online supplier or by calling 1-800-289-0963.